# Community Care in a Multi-Racial Britain:
## A CRITICAL REVIEW OF THE LITERATURE

Karl Atkin and
Janet Rollings

London: HMSO

ISBN 0 11 701758 2

This paper is based on work funded by the Department of Health but the
opinions expressed are those of the researchers alone.

*SPRU Editorial Group*
Sally Baldwin
Lorna Foster
Gillian Parker
Roy Sainsbury
Patricia Thornton
Peter Whiteford

Editor for this paper: Gillian Parker

British Library Cataloguing in Publication Data

A CIP catalogue record for this book is available from the British Library

# Acknowledgements

Our special thanks go to Gillian Parker who supervised this work and who, along with Chris Perring, made numerous helpful comments. We are grateful to Patricia Thornton and Lorna Foster for their contributions to draft versions of this monograph. We would also particularly like to thank Jenny Bowes who provided indispensable support.

The research was commissioned and funded by the Department of Health.

# Contents

List of tables    vii

Chapter One: Introduction    1
   The policy context    1
   The purpose and scope of the review    2
   The language of race    2
   Content of the review    4

Chapter Two: Ethnicity, disability and informal care    7
   Ethnicity    7
   Disability    9
   Informal care    11
   Conclusions    18

Chapter Three: Knowledge and use of statutory community
   service provision    19
   Introduction    19
   Social Service provision    20
   Community health service provision    25
   Conclusions    28

Chapter Four: Statutory community service provision: policy
   and practice    29
   The idea of cultural diversity    30
   Social services: policy and practice    32
   Health authorities: policy and practice    34
   Conclusions    40

Chapter Five: Employment, ethnic monitoring and interpret-
   ing services: a partial response    41
   Employment    41
   Ethnic monitoring    45
   Interpreting services    47
   Conclusions    48

Chapter Six: A way forward for statutory policy and practice    49
   Social services departments    49

Health authorities                                              51
Conclusions                                                     52

Chapter Seven: Voluntary provision                              53
  Knowledge and use of voluntary agencies                       53
  Policy and practice                                           54
  Conclusions                                                    60

Chapter Eight: Recommendations for future research              63
  Ethnicity, disability and informal care                       63
  The experience of community service provision                 65
  Service delivery: policy and practice                         65
  Race research and policy: an anti-racist methodology          67
  Community care and race: an agenda for action                 70

Appendix: Key studies cited in the review                       73

Bibliography                                                     79

Index                                                            99

# List of tables

Chapter Two

Table 2.1   The composition of the black population of Britain      8

Table 2.2   Distribution of black populations in Britain by
Department of Health regions and metropolitan
areas                                                              9

Chapter Three

Table 3.1   People who did not know about services (per
cent)                                                            20

# Introduction

## The policy context

After many years of neglect, recent debates on community care are slowly beginning to recognise the potential significance of ethnicity in formulating policy (Audit Commission, 1986; Williams, 1989). Sir Roy Griffiths (1988), in his agenda for action on community care, argued that both policy and action need to respond to the multi-racial nature of British society. Following this, the Government White Paper on Community Care (1989) and subsequent NHS and Community Care Act (1990) identified people from ethnic minorities as having 'particular care needs'. Good community care will thus take account of the circumstances of minority communities, be sensitive to their needs, and be planned in consultation with them. The policy and practice guidance recommendations on black and ethnic minorities further enforce this.

Black people have become part of the policy debates on community care (Bottomley, 1993). What these developments mean for black minorities is, however, less clear. A report of a conference organised by the Social Services Inspectorate expressed disquiet about community care implementation failing to address the needs of ethnic minority communities (DH, 1991). Other writers described uncertainty, puzzlement and ignorance about what should be done (Pearson, 1988; McNaught, 1990; Naina Patel, 1990). Policy thus remains undeveloped and rarely goes beyond bland statements supporting the principles of racial equality while the mechanisms that might achieve race equality, and the principles that underlie them, remain unexplored.

With an estimated 2.57 million black people living in this country, Britain is a multi-racial society. Those responsible for planning and implementing social care policy, whether they work in central government, local authorities, health authorities or the voluntary sector cannot ignore this, particularly when community care is at a crossroads, with the exact pattern of future provision uncertain. Questions concerning the range, quality and accessibility of service provision are being raised. All those involved in social care are having to re-examine their roles, responsibilities and aims, both with regard to individual users and to the process of service delivery. Race must be a part of this debate, otherwise the opportunities for efficient, effective and equitable provision will be missed.

## The purpose and scope of the review

This book, by reviewing existing literature on community care and black communities, gives coherence to a fragmented literature, illustrates gaps in present understanding and generates a research agenda relevant to current policy concerns. The book reviews a mix of empirical studies and policy debates emerging from the literature, thereby examining the experience of community care within black communities and delivery of service support to black people.

The nature of available information on community care in black communities has determined the balance of this review, which confines itself to the experience of Asian and Afro/Caribbean people. Although the situation of, for example, Chinese and Vietnamese groups is similar, the review has confined itself, for pragmatic reasons, to the two largest black communities living in Britain. The small number of empirical studies undertaken on the situation of black people has resulted in an inclusive and comprehensive review which considers all empirical studies, despite methodoligical limitations, providing they produce useful insights. Most of the literature discusses and explores the policy issues rather than presenting research findings so the debate is speculative and exploratory, grounded at the level of theory, rather than empirical evidence. Furthermore, because most of the literature assumes an anti-racist stance, the material tends to be critical of statutory service provision, dwelling on the numerous examples of poor service delivery rather than the small number of instances of good practice.

## The language of race

The language of race receives considerable attention; few terms have uniform acceptance or consistent application and they are ever-changing. Anxiety about using incorrect or inappropriate terms can inhibit much-needed discussion. However, an informed application of words and terms can assist coherent thinking and improved communication of ideas and information. A reader unfamiliar with recent debates concerning race may find it helpful to have certain terms clarified here. This section introduces some terms used regularly throughout the review. They represent shorthand definitions which refer to a diverse and complex reality, but inform the reader of the ideas behind some of the terms applied in this review.

## Black minorities

For convenience the phrase 'black minorities' used in this review, refers to people of Asian and Afro/Caribbean origin[1]. Clarification, however, is necessary. It is important, for example, to recognise that many people from Asian or Afro/Caribbean groups do not always identify themselves as black. Some Asian people, for instance, object to the word black and argue that it confuses a number of ethnic groups. Neither does the term imply that black minorities are a homogeneous group. They do share, however, a common experience of discrimination and inequality because of their ethnic origin, language, culture or religion. The term is political rather than analytical, and refers to Asian and Afro/Caribbean people who experience the effects of racism.

## Afro/Caribbean

This refers to persons of African origin born in one of the Caribbean Islands. It also includes their descendants born in the United Kingdom. It is a positive term of identity associated with a commitment to anti-racism.

## Asian

This refers to persons born in India, Pakistan or Bangladesh or the descendants of such territories born in East Africa. It also includes descendants born in the United Kingdom. Under certain circumstances it is inappropriate to bracket together such a wide variety of different cultural and ethnic groups. There is no one Asian culture but a series of Asian cultures. There are similarities, as with European culture, in that they share a similar foundation, but there is also great diversity. The term 'Asian', therefore, should either have a plural application (that is, Asian communities) or refer to the specific place of origin (for example, people from Pakistan).

## Race and ethnicity

There is an important distinction between these two words. The term 'race' was originally associated with social Darwinism and thus often regarded as derisive. More recently, however, the term is applied in an anti-racist sense, as a way of describing issues of ethnicity in the context of power relations. The notion of race, therefore, includes the social, economic and political position of black people. (This review applies the term in this way.) The term 'ethnicity' refers to cultural groups of various kinds without reference to their social, economic and political background.

Ethnicity is applied wrongly if it refers exclusively to people who form black minorities. All groups, including white, are ethnic. To avoid

---

[1]Usually the term black refers to people who identify themselves, or are identified as being of Afro/Caribbean, Indian, Pakistani, Bangladeshi, as well as Arabic, Vietnamese or Chinese origin or descent.

confusion it is best to be explicit about the ethnic group being discussed. General terms, such as ethnic minorities, however, are acceptable in that they refer to a minority ethnic group.

## Racism

All people hold prejudiced beliefs about people whom they see as different because of their origins or ethnic groups, but 'racism' can be attributed only to those who have the power to turn the prejudice into acts of discrimination or unfair treatment. Acts of discrimination can be conscious or unconscious and racism operates at two different levels, individual and institutional.

'Individual racism' occurs when a white person treats a black person unfairly because of their racial or ethnic origins. 'Institutional racism' is embedded in the operational practices of an organisation and includes, for example:

- service provision organised, by default, around a white norm. A day centre might only provide English food. This might ignore the preference of black clients.

- white service providers basing decisions on racist assumptions, stereotypes and myths. The idea amongst service providers that black people 'look after their own' often prevents the offer of support.

- regulations that apply to all but have the effect of excluding black people while maintaining the privileged position of white people. For example, waiting lists for local authority housing often exclude people who have not lived in an area for a number of years.

## Content of the review

The review is in ten parts. The introduction has outlined the policy relevance of the review and specified the terminology used in it. Chapter Two introduces empirical data and explores the situation and experience of black people: using demographic material it first describes the character of black communities living in Britain; and secondly discusses the experience of disability and informal care.

The next four chapters discuss the provision of statutory services to people who form black minorities. Chapter Three explores the preceptions of black people and their experience of community service provision. Chapters Four, Five and Six look at statutory provision and discuss the organisation and delivery of services to people who form black minorities. Chapter Seven discusses voluntary provision.

Chapter Eight offers an overview of the literature; it also looks at recommended changes in provision and outlines an agenda for future research. Finally, an Appendix describes the key studies cited in the review.

# Ethnicity, disability and informal care

To understand the context of community care among black minorities it is necessary to explore three features:

- the demographic character of black minorities living in the United Kingdom;
- the nature and experience of disability;
- the circumstances of informal care.

## Ethnicity

Along with economic factors, demographic change has a powerful influence on policy formulation and there are five aspects of this change which are relevant to the policy debate on social care. The first of these concerns the number of people from black and ethnic minorities, and demonstrates the multi-racial nature of British society. The second includes the composition of Britain's black population, and illustrates that black people are not an homogeneous group. Thirdly, the relationship between age and disability indicates the importance of the age distribution of black minority communities. Fourthly, differences between the numbers of males and females affect the population of those who need care, and of those who take on the responsibility of caring. Finally, the distribution of black people between localities is fundamental to planning community services; areas with high numbers of black people raise different planning and service delivery issues from those areas with low numbers of black people (Young, 1990).

According to the annual Labour Force Survey, during the period 1987–89 about 2.57 million (4.7 per cent) of the total population in Britain were from ethnic minorities. Fifty per cent of these people were born in Britain. South Asian (Indian, Pakistani and Bangladeshi) people comprised over half the total black minority population, while Afro/Caribbean people made up just under a quarter. The Indian communities were the largest single minority group in Britain. Table 2.1 gives the composition of Britain's black minority population (Haskey, 1991).

**Table 2.1   The composition of the black population of Britain**

| Ethnic group | Per cent |
|---|---|
| Bangladeshi | 4 |
| Indian | 30 |
| Pakistani | 17 |
| Afro/Caribbean | 19 |
| African | 5 |
| Chinese | 5 |
| Arab | 3 |
| Mixed | 11 |
| Other | 6 |

*Source*: Haskey, 1991

Minority groups are, on average, younger than the white population. Whereas a fifth of all private households in Great Britain contain a person aged 60 and over, this is the case for only four per cent of South Asian and six per cent of Afro/Caribbean people (Williams, 1990). Demographic trends, however, indicate an imminent growth in the numbers of older people of Afro/Caribbean and South East Asian descent (Cameron *et al.*, 1989a). The rising proportion of older people of Afro/Caribbean people (19 per cent) and Asian people (12 per cent), for example, is comparable to that of white people (19 per cent) (Williams, 1990). A difference in the age structure of the various ethnic minority groups, resulting from the patterns of migration from the respective countries of origin, also occurs. Bangladeshi and Pakistani communities, for instance, are generally younger, as people from these two countries have a shorter history of migration to Britain than Indian and Afro/Caribbean people.

An important gender imbalance characteristics the elderly population of black communities. According to Fenton (1987), men will outnumber women among black older people because of the differences in migration patterns. This is the reverse of the situation among the white population.

Another noticeable feature of black populations is their uneven distribution throughout Britain. The highest populations generally occur in London and the metropolitan counties, and the lowest in the non-metropolitan counties, particularly those in the South West, the North and Wales. Table 2.2 gives the distribution of black populations in Britian according to Department of Health regions and metropolitan areas (Haskey, 1991).

Table 2.2    Distribution of black populations in Britain by
Department of Health regions and metropolitan areas

| Region | Per cent of total population |
| --- | --- |
| Scotland | 0.9 |
| Wales | 1.2 |
| Tyne and Wear | 1.8 |
| Northern | 0.7 |
| North West | 2.2 |
| Greater Manchester | 5.2 |
| Merseyside | 2.0 |
| West Yorkshire | 8.0 |
| South Yorkshire | 2.2 |
| Yorkshire and Humberside | 4.2 |
| West Midlands | 2.0 |
| West Midlands (Metropolitan area) | 12.5 |
| East Midlands | 4.0 |
| North London | 3.0 |
| Greater London | 16.6 |
| Southern | 2.9 |
| South West | 1.2 |

Source: Haskey, 1991

The proportion of black people also varies greatly between local authorities. The London Borough of Brent, for instance, estimates that 27 per cent of its population is black. For York on the other hand the number is less than one per cent. Even within local authorities black people are found in particular localities. In Sparkbrook (Birmingham) for example, 50 per cent of the population is black, the majority being of South Asian origin. In the west of the city, Handsworth has a similarly high population of black people, although the majority are of Afro/Caribbean descent. Other areas of Birmingham, such as Sutton Coldfield, have fewer than one per cent of their total population classified as black (OPCS, 1983).

## Disability

One in seven of the British adult population is classified as disabled (Martin *et al.*, 1988) but there are only a few studies describing the extent or nature of disability among black people (McAvoy and Donaldson, 1990; McDonald, 1991). Research and planning have often been preoccupied with specific problems such as rickets, osteomalacia, thalassaemia, sickle cell anaemia and tuberculosis (Donovan, 1984; Pearson, 1986; Bhopal and Donaldson, 1988; Ahmad *et al.*, 1989). Although these diseases require specialised services, they affect relatively few people and may deflect attention away from more widespread need.

The number of surveys assessing the incidence of disability in black people, however, is slowly growing (RADAR, 1984; Donaldson and Odell, 1986; Farrah, 1986; Holland and Lewando-Hundt, 1987; GLAD, 1987). Tameside's (1987) survey of 186 Asian people, aged 50 or over, found physical difficulties increasing with age. Farrah (1986) demonstrated that 34 per cent of Afro/Caribbean people aged 55 or over reported a health problem that restricted daily activity; and the numbers reporting difficulty in self-care and domestic tasks were higher than described in the General Household Survey (Green, 1988). Donaldson and Odell's (1986) study of 726 older Asian people, aged 65 or over, and Holland and Lewando-Hundt's (1987) survey of 71 Afro/Caribbeans and 1163 Asians, aged 55 and over, produced similar findings.

Although some studies have suggested the incidence of disability was higher among black people than white people (Anwal Bhalla and Blakemore, 1981; Norman, 1985; Farrah, 1986; Fenton, 1987; Shabira Moledina, 1988; Ebrahim *et al.*, 1991) data from the OPCS survey of physical disability (Martin *et al.*, 1988) showed that, when standardised for age, the prevalence of disability amongst Afro/Caribbean and Asian people, compared with that amongst the white population, was roughly the same.

In comparison to physical disability there is little information on the nature and extent of black people with learning difficulties and mental health problems or on people with hearing and visual impairments. Methodological issues further complicate the issue. Data on the extent of problems associated with mental health, for instance, are problematic because of cultural bias in diagnosis (Ineichen, 1989; Cope, 1989; Knowles, 1991).

## The experience of disability

The literature acknowledges the importance of race in structuring a person's experience of disability and illness (Kiple and King, 1981; Pearson, 1983a; Currer, 1986; Donovan, 1986; Cameron *et al.*, 1989a; Oliver, 1991). There is little empirical work, however, that examines the relationship between black people's experience of health, illness and disability and the nature of community care. As a result we still do not have an adequate account of what disability means to black minorities.

The literature that is available explores the connection between disability and structural disadvantage faced by people who form black and ethnic minorities (Anwal Bhalla and Blakemore, 1981; Townsend and Davidson, 1982; Norman, 1985; Farrah, 1986; Fenton, 1987; Whitehead, 1987; Confederation of Indian Organisations, 1988; Shabira Moledina, 1988; Nasa Begum, 1992; Neelam Sharma, 1992). Norman (1985) suggests that the conditions in which black people live contribute to poor health and cites examples such as long hours of work in semi- or unskilled manual work. Black people are found in higher concentrations in manual and unskilled occupations than are white people (Holland and Lewando-Hundt, 1987), and these occupations have a higher incidence of health problems than other social groups (Townsend and Davidson, 1982). A report from the Policy Studies Institute describes the persistence of inequality for black people in respect of incomes, unemployment rates and poor housing. All three factors are related to ill-health (Brown, 1984).

It has been argued that black, disabled identity can only be understood within the context of institutional racism (Oliver, 1991). Black disabled people therefore seem to face a double disadvantage: that of being both black and disabled (Confederation of Indian Organisations, 1987; Nathwani, 1987).

## Informal care

The General Household Survey estimated that 6.7 million people care for sick, elderly or disabled people, within the same household (Green, 1988). These statistics, however, give no information about the number and circumstances of carers from black and ethnic minority groups, nor is there any other information source. Available information on informal care among black communities is limited to a few small-scale studies.

Information on caregiving among black communities is most often provided by local authority surveys. These, however, are locally based making generalisations difficult (Bradford Social Services, 1989; Tameside Metropolitan Council, 1989; London Borough of Camden, 1990; Brent Social Services, 1991; Nasa Begum, 1992). Farrah's (1986) survey of 109 Afro/Caribbean people aged 55 years and over suggested that 21 per cent were responsible for the care of others. Given the nature of survey work, which usually under-represents black communities, it is possible that these figures also under-estimate the extent of informal care.

McCalman (1990) is one of the few authors who has undertaken a survey of informal carers from black and ethnic minorities. Despite the difficulties of obtaining a sample she contacted 34 carers, living in the London Borough of Southwark. All the carers looked after a close relative; just over half a parent, step-parent or parent-in-law, one-third a spouse, and just over an eighth grandparents. Twenty-one carers were female. In exploring the tasks undertaken by black carers McCalman found that 21 carers undertook some kind of personal care, and 24 provided physical help such as lifting or walking. All the carers reported substantial time spent in caring activities; 25 carers, for example, spent over 11 hours per day caring for older relatives. Carers also reported that they had spent a considerable amount of their lives caring; five had been caring for 11 years and 28 for over two years.

## The experience of informal care

As for white people, care in the community for black families usually means care by the family. However, in comparison with what is known about white carers, there is little information on the experience of informal care among black communities. Available information is speculative and exploratory, based on small-scale studies. Detailed information is, therefore, sparse. There is little material, for instance, on the experience of caring for people with different types of disabilities. Nor is there any attempt to distinguish between different types of caregiving. Nonetheless the literature does outline potential policy concerns. Further research would help substantiate these.

### The visibility of black carers

The invisible nature of caregiving is well established for white population (Twigg and Atkin, 1993) and these problems seem intensified for black people (Jones, 1990). Not only do they face the general invisibility of informal carers, but also the neglect brought about by their ethnic origin (Lee, 1987; Cole, 1990; Jowell et al., 1990; Dourado, 1991; Wallace, 1991; Yee, 1991; Meena Patel, 1991; Nasa Begum, 1992; Wilson, 1992). Baxter (1988) described black people as the 'invisible carers' and Hicks (1988a) as 'one of the most neglected and invisible groups in the country'. Two recent initiatives, however, raise the profile of black carers.

First, the Carers Unit of the King's Fund, established in 1986, recognised the need to include the specific issues faced by black carers as an integral part of its work (Lunn, 1990; Yee, 1991; Wilson, 1992). As a starting point all projects incorporated black issues (Richardson et al., 1989). The Unit set up a forum, to increase the visibility of black and ethnic minority carers, and initiated two projects. One project produced a video and leaflets providing information to help Asian carers in Leicester (Saroj Bulsara, 1988; Bould, 1990a). The second project was McCalman's small-scale study of Asian, Afro/Caribbean and Chinese carers in Southwark (1990). The King's Fund has since initiated more, locally based projects which seek out carers from ethnic minority communities and ask them about their needs (Wilson, 1992);

reports include a study of 33 Asian carers mainly in London, Birmingham, Bradford and Derbyshire (Gunaratnum, 1990), and a further small-scale study of Afro/Caribbean carers (Eribo, 1991).

The second initiative is the Birmingham Community Care Special Action Project (CCSAP), established in 1987, which aimed to improve support for black carers. The CCSAP obtained a grant from the King's Fund to undertake a short-term enquiry into the needs of black and ethnic minority carers, and produce policy guidelines, which would give practical guidance on developing consultation with carers in black and ethnic minority communities (Jowell *et al.*, 1990).

## Who cares?

Parker (1990) argues that one of the most persistent misconceptions about 'modern society' is that the family no longer cares for disabled and older people. This, however is not an argument usually applied to black, and particularly Asian, families. Indeed, their commitment to care for older and disabled relatives is assumed to be greater than that of white people, to the extent that service provision thinks it need not concern itself with black people's needs. Our aim here is to evaluate this assumption, critically, identify where care is based, and explore who does the caring.

## Family networks: myths and reality

Research into the circumstances of black families suggests the supportive extended family network is largely a myth. Cancerlink, for example, argued that there is a commonly held view that Asian people look after their own, and have self-supporting extended family networks. Perhaps the most revealing finding of their research, they concluded, was the shattering of these assumptions (Baxter, 1989a).

The organisation of Asian families tends to be bi-modal. Although the extended family is common among Asian families (Barker, 1984), there is still a significant proportion of Asian people who live alone, with few relatives in this country (Atkin *et al.*, 1989a). Fenton (1987) concluded that 'extended families were common, but by no means universal'. Anwal Bhalla and Blakemore (1981) suggested that only five per cent of older Asian people live alone, although they added that 26 per cent in their study had no family in Britain outside their immediate household. Atkin *et al.* (1989a), similarly, reported that older Asian people were more likely to live in extended families than their white counterparts. Some four per cent of Asian older people lived alone compared to 44 per cent of white older people, and 51 per cent of Asian older people lived in three generational households, compared to six per cent of the white sample. Atkin *et al.* (1989a) concluded, however, that service providers should remember that many Asian people do live alone, and described the situation of Yusif Uddin to illustrate this:

Yusif Uddin, a Muslim aged 64, originally came to Britain from Pakistan, in 1958, to look for work. He was employed in manual work, but after being made redundant in 1980, he returned to Pakistan. He came back to Britain in 1982, and has been unemployed since then. He lives alone in a rented Edwardian inner city terrace house which is damp and in need of basic repair. His only form of heating comes from a gas fire. His wife and son live in Pakistan at present, although he is waiting for them to come over and join him. The waiting, he says, causes him a great deal of anxiety and worry and he feels lonely and isolated. His health is not good and he has respiratory problems and mobility difficulties. As a result of this he cannot take adequate care of himself or the house.

The traditional pattern in many Asian communities, of sharing the responsibility for care among a network of family members, is not so applicable in Britain (Cameron et al., 1989a). Fenton (1987) for instance, pointed out that migration itself divides many migrant families and this has been exacerbated by post-1962 legislation and the administration of immigration policy. Cameron et al. (1989a) concluded that changes in family structure and household structure, and the geographical dispersal of close and extended kin made it difficult for the extended family network to offer support for older and disabled relatives. Changing family structure and housing problems led to difficulties despite continuing strong feelings of obligation (Lalljie, 1983; London Borough of Camden, 1990).

Changing family structure can lead to what Bal Chauhan (1989) termed psychological jeopardy. He described the situation of older black people who have looked after their parents and in turn expect to be looked after by their offspring. If this expectation were not fully realised the older person might experience shock, disappointment, shame or loss (Coombe, 1981; Shabira Moledina, 1988). The changing role relationship in Asian families is often a source of stress. Fenton (1987) described 'inescapable tensions' of some older Asian people who found it difficult to comprehend changes which had occurred in the attitudes and life styles of their sons and daughters. Cameron et al. (1989a) observed the 'conflicting expectations' of different generations and the role conflict which results.

The large extended family is uncommon among Afro/Caribbean families (Barker, 1984). Anwal Bhalla and Blakemore (1981) reported that over a third of Afro/Caribbean people live alone while Farrah (1986) showed that although 88 per cent of Afro/Caribbeans had children, only 59 per cent had frequent family contact. Contact was diminished if the parent was disabled. The survey by Berry et al. (1981) of older Afro/Caribbean people suggested a third had either no children, or their children lived abroad. Fenton (1987) concluded that many older Afro/Caribbeans were not only isolated in a household sense, but also unsupported by contiguous other family members.

## Who cares within the family?

Regardless of the size or structure of the family network, research shows that, when caring responsibilities are taken on, as with white families, the locus of care is usually the immediate family (Lee, 1987; Cameron et al., 1989a; McCalman, 1990), and the main responsibility of care falls to one family member. McCalman (1990) observed, in her study of Asian and Afro/Caribbean families, that help received from other family members was incidental or occasional. Several carers received no help.

Again, as is the case in white families, women usually undertake the role of carers more than men (Walker, 1987; Janjit Uppal, 1988; Cameron et al., 1989a; Bould, 1990a; Cocking and Athwal, 1990; McCalman, 1990; London Borough of Camden, 1990). Walker (1987) identified 15 Asian families caring for a child with a severe learning difficulty; and the mother always assumed responsibility for all aspects of care. One cannot however, assume that different social groups perceive informal care in the same way. Atkin and Baldwin (1988) have suggested that, although women usually provide day-to-day care, some Asian groups identify caregiving with economic support and male heads of household are invariably defined as 'carers'.

## The physical cost of care

Carers experience a level of physical exertion in their daily living far above that experienced by other people (Parker, 1990). Many carers in the Southwark study referred to earlier found the physical burden of care too great and expressed the need for assistance with tasks such as lifting or bathing (McCalman, 1990). The report also found that many carers themselves were in ill health; the work of Farrah (1986) and Eribo (1991) support this. Other than this there is little information on the physical burden faced by black carers.

## The emotional cost of care

Research on white carers suggests that caring brings about increased levels of stress or emotional strain (Parker, 1990). Although there is a lack of systematic exploration of these issues in relation to black people, the small amount of evidence available suggests their experience of caring is similar (Walker, 1987; Eribo, 1991). However, the disadvantage associated with ethnicity appears to intensify their experience (Cameron et al., 1989a). The literature emphasises the isolation and loneliness of caring (Powell and Perkins, 1984; Watson, 1984; Holland and Lewando-Hundt, 1987; Janjit Uppal, 1988; McCalman, 1990; Eribo, 1991; Wallace, 1991). Barker (1984), for example, wrote that 'a sense of isolation pervades the comments of many black respondents'. Bould (1990a) described how many black carers felt trapped within four walls, with no alternative but to care. Over half of the carers spoke of experiencing depression. Gulliford (1984) concluded that Bangladeshi families looking after a child with a severe learning difficulty were more socially isolated and lacking in social support than carers in white families.

Women carers appeared to experience a greater sense of isolation and loneliness than men (Anwal Bhalla and Blakemore, 1981; Donovan, 1986; McAvoy, 1990; McCalman, 1990). This is similar to the situation of white female carers, although again racism seemed to compound this experience. Cameron et al. (1989a) concluded that black women carers were restricted to their houses through fear of an 'alien' outside world, where their own norms, values and social skills were often regarded as inappropriate and their behaviour in danger of misrepresentation.

Isolation is often made worse by communication difficulties (Cameron et al., 1989a), particularly for female rather than male carers (London Borough of Camden, 1990). Asian people speak many languages but for some, more often older people and women, English is not one of them. The Policy Studies Institute survey (Brown, 1984) reported that over half of Asian adults aged over 55 spoke little or no English, compared to about a quarter of adult Asians under 35. For all age groups, men are on the whole more fluent than women (Donaldson and Odell, 1986). Although some Afro/Caribbean speak patois, English is a first language for the majority. Communciation, however, is more than use of language, and Afro/Caribbean men and women may face barriers resulting from accents, dialect, the use of jargon and slang, and factors like pitch, speed, stress, intonation and rhythms. Non-verbal signs such as eye contact and body language are also important (Mares et al., 1985; Atkin et al., 1989a).

Other forms of emotional stress experienced by black carers include a lack of knowledge about the disabled person's condition (Walker, 1987; Cocking and Athwal, 1990; Baxter et al., 1990). McCalman (1990) reported that lack of knowledge made black carers feel insecure and undermined their confidence in providing appropriate care. Zamora (1988) described a similar feeling expressed by black carers looking after someone diagnosed as mentally ill.

Caring for a disabled person often causes strains within family life and in carers' relationships with the person they care for (McCalman, 1990). Bould (1990a) for example, described how Asian women looking after a disabled child often experienced tensions in their marriage, as well as finding it difficult to attend to the non-disabled children in the family. Similarly Pai and Kapur, in their 1981 study of the burden placed on the families of psychiatric patients, reported that for carers the most difficult part of their role was the disruption of normal family activities caused by looking after the relatives.

The emotional stress experienced by black carers often finds little relief and many black carers continue to provide care with little respite (Bould, 1990a; Eribo, 1991). McCalman (1990) described how only eight out of 34 carers had been on holiday since caring, while 15 could not remember when they had last had a holiday.

## The financial burden of care

Caring imposes economic costs. Some of these are on the expenditure side and arise directly out of the extra cost imposed by looking after a disabled person. Other costs are on the income side and arise principally from restricted employment.

The literature explores the financial difficulties associated with looking after a disabled person (Saroj Bulsara, 1988; McCalman, 1990; Bould, 1990a; Eribo, 1991). McCalman (1990) found that none of the eight Asian carers she interviewed was in employment, yet all these women had the responsibility of supporting their families financially because of the severity of their husbands' disability. They felt the burden of care would make it difficult for them to keep a job. In contrast, eight of the thirteen Afro/Caribbean carers interviewed were engaged in full-time work, with a further two in part-time employment. All stated they had to work to maintain themselves and the person they looked after. Social security benefits, they felt, were inadequate.[2] Black carers also lose educational opportunities and advancement at work (Bould, 1990a).

The financial costs of care appear similar to those experienced by the white population. Black people, however, are further disadvantaged as their incomes are likely to be lower than those of white people (Brown, 1984; Norman, 1985; Oppenheim, 1990). Gulliford (1984), for instance, concluded that Bangladeshi families, looking after a child with a severe mental handicap, experienced greater financial deprivation than white families.

## Housing

Although housing forms part of the environment of care, it has received relatively little attention in the mainstream carer literature and the role of housing in community care is generally neglected in policy discussion. There are, however, signs that the wider questions relating to the ways in which housing can facilitate or militate against community care are beginning to be addressed (Twigg, Atkin with Perring,

---

[2] The relationship between social care and social security, although an important aspect of community care provision, is outside the scope of this review.

1990; Oldman, 1990). There has been no systematic examination of housing issues in relation to black carers, although the available evidence suggests it is important.

Overall, the quality of housing for black people in this country is much worse than for white people (Brown, 1984; Phillips, 1987). Black people are more likely to live in flats, and these flats are more likely to be in high-rise blocks (Brown, 1984). Those with houses are less likely to live in detached or semi-detached property and their property is also likely to be older. Brown (1984) concluded that on average black people lived in smaller properties than white people and were more likely to experience overcrowding. In Southwark, for example, the person cared for was often unable to have a room of his or her own, and shared with other members of the family, often younger children (McCalman, 1990). In Donaldson and Odell's (1986) study in Leicester, 22 per cent of older Asian people interviewed shared a bedroom with someone else, usually a grandchild.

The lack of space also meant that some carers were unable to have their cared-for relative to live with them although they would have liked to be able to do this (McCalman, 1990). This created further problems for carers, including having to leave the relative alone, travelling costs (both time and money) and the responsibilities for maintaining two homes.

It is not surprising, therefore, that several studies have reported considerable housing problems for disabled people and carers from black minorities (Smith, 1988; Gunaratnum, 1990; McCalman, 1990; Standing Conference on Ethnic Minority Senior Citizens, 1991). Anwal Bhalla and Blakemore (1981) reported that 25 per cent of disabled Asian people and 33 per cent of disabled Afro/Caribbean people experienced housing problems and wanted to move. Farrah (1986) found similar dissatisfaction among older Afro/Caribbean people. Thirty per cent expressed a desire to move, and of these seven per cent needed single level accommodation and 12 per cent wanted improved toilet access.

## Conclusions

Over the next ten years demographic changes will increase pressure on the caring responsibilities of black families. There will be more older people living in the community and, because of the relationship between age, sex and disability, it seems there will be a corresponding increase in the numbers of people requiring care. Little is known, however, about the nature and experience of disability and informal care among black communities.

# Knowledge and use of statutory community service provision

## Introduction

The need for service provision which is racially sensitive has only recently been recognised (Norman, 1985; Naina Patel, 1990) and there is little empirical work examining how to incorporate black users' views into service delivery (Atkin, 1991b). The debate is thus still at the exploratory stage. Service provision to black people, for example, is often conceptualised in terms of knowledge and use of community-based health and personal social services and rarely considers the quality of service delivery.

The available literature demonstrates how little black people know about community services, irrespective of age or disability (Anwal Bhalla and Blakemore, 1981; Donaldson and Odell, 1986; Holland and Lewando-Hundt, 1987; Lee, 1987; Atkin et al., 1989a; Connelly, 1989; Baxter et al., 1990; Standing Conference of Ethnic Minority Senior Citizens, 1991). Holland and Lewando-Hundt (1987) for example, reported that 50 per cent of their Asian and Afro/Caribbean sample had heard of none of the social services listed. Knowledge of health services appears even poorer (Glendenning and Pearson, 1988; McAvoy and Donaldson, 1990). Atkin et al. (1989a) illustrated how a substantial proportion of older Asian people had not heard of various community health and social services; this was in direct contrast to the knowledge of the white sample (Table 3.1).

The literature suggests there is a difference between Asian and Afro/Caribbean communities' knowledge of services; with Afro/Caribbean older people better informed about social services than Asian older people (Anwal Bhalla and Blakemore, 1981; Holland and Lewando-Hundt, 1987; McCalman, 1990). Afro/Caribbean people's knowledge of community service is nonetheless limited (Raphael Phipps, cited Reba Bhaduri, 1988). Furthermore, although empirical studies suggest that Afro/Caribbean people's knowledge of services is greater than that of Asian communities, knowledge and receipt of services is significantly less than for white older people (Anwal Bhalla and Blakemore, 1981).

Table 3.1    **People who did not know about services (per cent)**

| Community Service | Proportion not knowing of each service | |
|---|---|---|
| | Asian (n = 81) | White (n = 55) |
| District Nurse | 57 | 14 |
| Nurse auxiliaries (bath nurse) | 76 | 32 |
| Chiropody | 64 | 9 |
| Home help | 62 | 1 |
| Meals on wheels | 58 | 0 |
| Social work | 44 | 6 |
| Day care | 60 | 18 |

*Source*: Atkin *et al.*, 1989a

The under use of community services among black people is well documented (Anwal Bhalla and Blakemore, 1981; Holland and Lewando-Hundt, 1987; Atkin *et al.*, 1989a). A survey in Birmingham, for example, found that approximately seven per cent of service users were black, although population statistics show that in the two wards covered by the survey 50 per cent of the population lived in households where the head was born in the New Commonwealth or Pakistan. Interviews with Asian and white people confirmed this. Three out of 33 disabled Asian people compared to 11 out of 33 disabled white people, for instance, received community nursing services. Health services generally had proportionately fewer black clients than did social services (Atkin *et al.*, 1989a).

Evidence suggests that black minorities often express an interest in using services once they know about them (Holland and Lewando-Hundt, 1987; Atkin *et al.*, 1989a). Atkin *et al.* (1989a) however, concluded that although a high proportion of Asian people would consider using a community-based service in future, with potential demand being slightly higher for community health services, there were often important provisos governing their willingness to use a service.

## Social Service provision

### Social work

The lack of knowledge of social work services among black minorities is well documented (Donaldson and Odell, 1986; Farrah, 1986;

McFarland *et al.*, 1989). McFarland *et al.* (1989) for example, found that 80 per cent of white people had some knowledge of social work services, compared with only 18 per cent of Asian people. Black minorities also have little contact with social workers (Donaldson and Odell, 1986). Of the 109 Afro/Caribbean people interviewed by Farrah (1986) only four people had used this service. Black people, however, are prepared to use the service. Atkin *et al.* (1989a) reported that 69 per cent of Asian people would consider using the service, compared to 74 per cent of the white population.

## Occupational therapy
As with most community services, black people know little about occupational therapy (Farrah, 1986; Shabira Moledina, 1988; McCalman, 1990). Again there appears to be a need for this service amongst black communities (McCalman, 1990; Farrah, 1986).

## Home help service
In McCalman's (1990) study of black carers, Asians carers' knowledge of domiciliary care services was slight – only two of eight Asians knew of the home help service, compared with 12 of 13 Afro/Caribbean carers. Larger studies also reflect the difference in knowledge of home help service between Asian and Afro/Caribbean people (Anwal Bhalla and Blakemore, 1981; Holland and Lewando-Hundt, 1987).

Asian and Afro/Caribbean people are less likely to use the home help service compared with white people (Anwal Bhalla and Blakemore, 1981; Holland and Lewando-Hundt, 1987). Again low take-up of a service is not necessarily a reflection of expressed low need among black minorities. Survey results show a willingness among black and ethnic minority people to use the home help service once it is explained to them (Holland and Lewando-Hundt, 1987; Shabira Moledina, 1988; McFarland *et al.*, 1989; Atkin *et al.*, 1989a), with those living alone or in one generational households expressing the greatest need (Donaldson and Odell, 1986). Asian older people are, however, less inclined to use the service in comparison to white people (Atkin *et al.*, 1989a). The lack of Asian home helps appeared to be a major reservation for Asian people when considering using the service (Holland and Lewando-Hundt, 1987; Shabira Moledina, 1988; Jowell *et al.*, 1990; McCalman, 1990; Wallace, 1991).

## Meals-on-wheels
Ethnic minority communities know less about meals-on-wheels than white people (Atkin *et al.*, 1989a). There are also differences between Asian and Afro/Caribbean minorities (Holland and Lewando-Hundt, 1987; McCalman, 1990). Anwal Bhalla and Blakemore (1981), for example, reported that 80 per cent of Afro/Caribbean people knew of

the service compared to 13 per cent of Asian people and 96 per cent of white people.

Receipt of the service was low for both Afro/Caribbean and Asian communities (Donaldson and Odell, 1986; Farrah, 1986; Holland and Lewando-Hundt, 1987). Black people, however, have expressed a need for meals-on-wheels (Farrah, 1986; Atkin et al., 1989a). Nonetheless, McFarland et al. (1989) report that, although most of the Asian people they interviewed felt the services would be of help, there was apprehension about the kind of meals provided. This apprehension is perhaps not surprising as food is central to many people's source of beliefs and identity (Levi-Strauss, 1970). Meals-on-wheels largely reflect white cultural beliefs. The literature raises issues of content/type, vegetarian/Halal meat, methods of preparation, styles of cooking and hygiene standards (Holland and Lewando-Hundt, 1987; Tameside Metropolitan Borough Council, 1987; Atkin et al., 1989a; Cole, 1990; Jowell et al., 1990; Naina Patel 1990; Wallace, 1991).

Where local authorities have recognised need and provided appropriate meals services, provision has been over-subscribed. In 1986, for example, a Muslim meals service was established in Liverpool. Prior to this a very small number of black people received the local authority's meals-on-wheels service. Although the project originally intended to provide 25 meals a day, five days a week, demand was so great that the service was soon providing between 36 and 38 daily meals, including deliveries on Saturday (Rooney, 1987).

### Luncheon clubs

Evidence suggests that more Afro/Caribbean than Asian people know of luncheon clubs (Holland and Lewando-Hundt, 1987; McCalman, 1990). However, take-up of the service amongst black people is low (Turnbull, 1985; Farrah, 1986: Holland and Lewando-Hundt, 1987; London Borough of Camden, 1990). Black people express similar reservations about luncheon clubs as they do about meals-on-wheels. With a few exceptions the type of food and social activities at luncheon clubs remain ethnocentric, reflecting white cultural beliefs (Farrah, 1986; Rooney, 1987).

### Day care

Knowledge of day care provision is generally limited among black minorities (Donaldson and Odell, 1986; Atkin et al., 1989a), but is usually greater among Afro/Caribbean people (Holland and Lewando-Hundt, 1987; McCalman, 1990).

Although only a small number of black minority people attend day centres (Holland and Lewando-Hundt, 1987; Rooney, 1987), evidence suggests that when Afro/Caribbean and Asian people know of services, considerable demand exists (Anwal Bhalla and Blakemore, 1981;

Donaldson and Odell, 1986; Holland and Lewando-Hundt, 1987; Atkin *et al.*, 1989a). This level of demand amongst black communities appears similar to that of white people (Atkin *et al.*, 1989a) with no significant difference expressed between those who live alone or in one generation households, and those who live in multi-generation households (Donaldson and Odell, 1986).

Reservations about using day care, however, have been noted among black minorities (Anwal Bhalla and Blakemore, 1981; Heptinstall, 1989; Naina Patel, 1990). These included concern over speaking and under-standing English; concern over the type of food offered and the catering arrangements; and inability to participate fully in leisure pursuits because of health/physical reasons. Many black people, for example, expressed reluctance to attend a day centre because they felt they might be the only black person there (Reba Bhaduri, 1988; Jowell *et al.*, 1990; Naina Patel, 1990). Lee (1987) interviewed black families with a member who had a learning disability. There were many positive comments about the service but also some negative ones. The most frequently occurring complaint was the absence of culturally appropri-ate food, such as Halal meat or vegetarian meals. The other commonly mentioned problem related to lack of shared language, and consequent communication difficulties.

Due to inadequate provision within mainstream services there is an increasing number of black voluntary groups who run their own day centres (Daniel, 1988; Heptinstall, 1989; Standing Conference on Ethnic Minority Senior Citizens, 1991). Most Asian day centres, however, cater for men rather than women (Norman, 1985; Holland and Lewando-Hundt, 1987; London Borough of Camden, 1990). The problems facing black voluntary groups are explored in more detail in Chapter Seven.

## Institutional and family respite care

Little empirical evidence exists about knowledge and use of respite care services by black and ethnic minority groups. What evidence there is suggests knowledge of respite services is low among black com-munities (Farrah, 1986; McCalman, 1990; Cole, 1990; Cocking and Athwal, 1990; Robinson and Stalker, 1992). Farrah (1986), for example, concluded that significantly fewer people knew about respite care than any of the other community services listed in the study.

There does, however, seem to be a need for respite services among Asian and Afro/Caribbean carers (Walker, 1987; Fielding, 1990; Poonia and Ward, 1990). Robinson and Stalker (1992) for example, reported that expressed need for respite service was twice as high for Asian families as for white families. Many of the anxieties black carers feel about respite care are, however, similar to those expressed by white carers (Twigg, 1989; Parker, 1990). Robinson's study reported that 73 per cent of parents expressed guilt or apprehension about their disabled child staying away from home for the first time (cited in Poonia and Ward, 1990). An Asian parent commented:

> It took us some time before we could put our child in a home, thinking he would be away from home and somebody looking after him. That took us a long time to make a decision because every time I told my wife 'Let go and put Sandeep in a home', she was . . . the tears all the time, and she said no because it would be very difficult for us at home not seeing Sandeep every moment. After a long time we made a decision – we shall put him in a home for a day, and now we found out it helps us a lot. (*Caring and Sharing* – a video produced by King's Fund and Health Education Authority, 1989)

Many ethnic minority families appear reluctant to use short-term care in its present form (Lee, 1987). Black carers are uneasy about how their children will fare in a strange environment organised around white norms. There appears to be an overwhelming feeling among Asian communities that services are not geared towards their needs, with many carers feeling that religious and other cultural practices are not considered (Baxter, 1989a; Poonia and Ward, 1990). For example, a common perception among many black parents participating in a family respite scheme in Lewisham, was that the scheme was a white organisation, working for white families (Contact A Family, 1989). Similarly, Lee's study (1987) of black families with a member who had a learning disability showed a preference for 'same race' placements.

In general three reasons explain low take-up: lack of information and communication; concerns about how black children will be looked after; and limited availability of black carers and professionals. Bould (1990b), for example, suggested that care attendants and respite services are not familiar with the cultural or religious needs of black users nor able to communicate in a common language. Robinson (1988) adopted a similar theme, by describing the information and communication difficulties faced by ethnic minority families in the use of respite care (Poonia and Ward, 1990).

## Sitting services and Crossroads Care Attendant schemes
There are no figures available on the use by black and ethnic minorities of respite services provided by voluntary agencies such as Crossroads Care Attendant schemes. Nor is there much information on black people's knowledge of the service. The London Borough of Camden report (1990) concluded that users who do not speak English are unlikely to have heard about Crossroads. This report was also one of the few studies to address the issue of 'sitting services' and described the reservations expressed by black carers. These were similar to the reservations expressed in the general literature on respite services and

included a lack of trust in leaving their relative with a stranger and anxiety about having a stranger in the house in their absence. The shortage of care attendants from the same ethnic and cultural background able to communicate with the person being cared for exacerbated these reservations.

## Carer support groups

Carer support groups are one of the few forms of support directly focused on informal carers. The forms of activity and organisation encompassed by carer support groups are diverse and include groups organised professionally by social workers or health practitioners, as well as groups run by carers for carers. Some groups are generic, attracting all types of carers, others focus on specific client groups.

The benefits to carers of carer support groups are well recognised (Twigg *et al.*, 1990). Characteristically, the groups offer a mixture of social and emotional support, and information sessions. In the past, use of these groups appeared limited among black people, although the growth of groups catering specifically for the needs of black people indicates their increasing importance (Baxter *et al.*, 1990; Bould, 1990b; Fielding, 1990; Eribo, 1991; Wallace, 1991).

## Community health service provision

### General Practice

Registration with a general practitioner is similar for all ethnic groups. A large-scale household survey carried out in the West Midlands in 1981, reported that 99 per cent of white, Asian and Afro/Caribbean people were registered with a general practitioner (Johnson, 1986). This percentage was similar to the findings presented by Fenton (1987). As a result of language and communication difficulties with white general practitioners many Asian patients prefer to register with a GP of Asian origin (Donovan, 1986; Johnson, 1986).

The use of a general practitioner by black people is higher than in white communities (Blakemore, 1982; Barker, 1984; Johnson, 1986). Donaldson and Odell (1986), for example, showed that 92 per cent of the Asian older people interviewed had consulted a GP at least once in previous six months, compared with 63 per cent of white older people. Information for younger black and white people's contact with general practice seemed to suggest similar patterns of consultation (Norman, 1985).

This higher rate of GP consultation among black minorities has led several studies to examine whether ethnic minority clients made excessive or unjustified demands on the health services (Johnson,

1986). Evidence does not substantiate such suggestions and some authors propose that high consultation rates among black people might be the result of cultural factors (Fennell *et al.*, 1989). Other authors, however, are critical of the notion of cultural differences in explaining differences in consultation rates, and point out that black people often face poorer health due to disadvantage (Johnson, 1986; Fenton, 1987; Gillam *et al.*, 1989). To understand higher consultation rates, research needs to explain health inequalities within a flexible framework, which accommodates factors such as disadvantages in employment, housing, education, the effects of migration, and changing lifestyles from one generation to the next, as well as direct and indirect discrimination. Since few relevant community surveys have been carried out, it is difficult to know the extent to which different patterns of consultation reflect real differences in health or the differing perceptions of illness and differing expectations about doctors.

There is little detailed information on the experience of general practice for black minorities. Donovan (1986) looked at the health experiences and perceptions of Asian and Afro/Caribbean patients including their views of general practice. The Asian patients tended to rely on their general practitioners, whereas the Afro/Caribbean patients inclined to have a general scepticism about the ability of doctors and drugs to effect cures and, therefore, used them mainly as 'a last resort'. Most of the Asian and Afro/Caribbean patients in the sample were not critical of their general practitioners, but they did complain about too brief consultations, the seemingly automatic providing of prescriptions, doctors' failure to carry out adequate examinations, and the length of time they had to wait. Wilkin and Williams (1986) reported that the experience of white people was similar.

The different treatment of ethnic groups by general practitioners has been a feature of the literature in this field. Gillam *et al.* (1989) found that white patients were much more likely to leave the surgery with a follow-up appointment than Asian or Afro/Caribbean people.

Taylor and Maynard (1990) suggest that general practitioners are more reluctant to give prescriptions to Afro/Caribbean and Asian families than they are to white families. Anwhal Bhalla and Blakemore (1981) found that the proportion of Asian and Afro/Caribbean people who did not receive treatment for ailments affecting their eyes, feet, ears and teeth was higher than that of white people not receiving treatment when they reported similar problems. Atkin *et al.* (1989b) also found that general practitioners were less likely to refer disabled Asian patients than white patients to district nursing services.

## Community nursing services
Apart from general practice, black minorities know little about other community-based health service practitioners (Norman, 1985; Shabira

Moledina, 1988). Although Afro/Caribbean people seemed to have similar knowledge of community nursing to that of white people (McCalman, 1990), fewer Asian people had heard of the service (Atkin *et al.*, 1989a).

Once aware of the role of the service Asian older people were just as likely as white older people to consider using community nursing services (Atkin *et al.*, 1989a). Asian people who express a need for community nursing service have reservations, however (Shabira Moledina, 1988; Atkin *et al.*, 1989a). Muslim men, for example, expressed a strong preference for a male bath nurse (Atkin *et al.*, 1989a).

Black people's experience of community nursing services in some ways is similar to that of white people. The dissatisfactions expressed by black people include nurses' unreliability, and their breaking appointments without explanation, always being late, and having little time to spend in the house (Evers *et al.*, 1989). White people describe similar dissatisfactions (Twigg and Atkin, 1993). Black people, however, tend to face further difficulties. The findings of Badger *et al.* (1990) in a study of people suffering from dementia and mental impairment, revealed that contact with the health service was less common for the ethnic minority group than for the random white sample. The nine Asian and Afro/Caribbean dementia clients identified in the sample were not judged to need additional nursing services to the same extent as the white sample – and this was despite the fact that they were more disabled physically. None of the nine clients had requested services in the past year compared to nearly three-quarters of the whole sample. The authors acknowledged that small numbers made analysis difficult, but suggested that a variety of factors, such as the prevalence of stereotypes and myths held by community nurses, resulted in clients' and carers' perceptions and needs not being fully explored.

## Other community health services

Other community health services receive little attention in the literature. There is only one study that discusses the role of community psychiatric nurses (McCalman, 1990) which reported that only three out of 21 Afro/Caribbean and Asian carers knew about the service, and none had contact with it.

McCalman's (1990) study also provided information on continence services. She reported that five out of 13 Afro/Caribbean carers had heard of the service compared to none of the eight Asian carers. Only one older Afro/Caribbean relative received the care of a continence adviser. Yet the sample reveals that two Afro/Caribbean and one Asian relative were completely incontinent, while five Afro/Caribbean and three Asian relatives had occasional problems. The Foleshill Mental Handicap Survey – which interviewed 38 families containing a member with severe learning difficulties, 23 of whom were of Asian origin –

revealed similar results. Twenty-three people in the study were incontinent, yet only six of their families knew of the incontinence laundry
scheme which existed in that area (Cocking and Athwal, 1990).

McCalman (1990) has also provided the only available information on
rehabilitation services. Six Afro/Caribbean carers but none of the
Asian carers had heard of the physiotherapy services; and only two
Afro/Caribbean older relatives used it. Speech therapy was known to
five Afro/Caribbean carers and one Asian carer, and had been used by
one older Asian person.

With regard to chiropody, empirical evidence suggests that older Asian
and Afro/Caribbean people rarely know of the service (Farrah, 1986;
Donaldson and Odell, 1986; Shabira Moledina, 1988; Atkin et al., 1989a;
McCalman, 1990) although once aware of it black people are as likely as
white people to consider using it (Atkin et al., 1989a).

## Conclusions

There is little empirical work examining how to incorporate black user
views into service delivery. The debate is still at an exploratory stage
and conceptualises the issue in terms of knowledge and use of community services. Despite the limitations of the data three important
points emerge. First, there is a low level of knowledge of community
services among black people and this appears to be irrespective of age
and disability. Secondly, there is an under use of services among black
people. Thirdly, although important provisos govern their willingness
to use a service, black minorities are interested in using services once
they know about them.

# Statutory community service provision: policy and practice

The last chapter outlined research on black communities' experience of community service provision. This chapter, and the following two, place this information in a wider context by exploring the policy and practice of statutory service provision to people who form black minorities. Two features of the literature determine the scope of these chapters. First, there has been no systematic exploration of the relationship between service delivery and black people. Few large-scale empirical studies exist and much of the literature discusses and explores the policy issues rather than presenting research findings. Secondly, the literature is parochial, structured according to particular service sectors. Although general principles such as institutional racism are applicable to both sectors, no account examines the service system as a whole. However it is encouraging to report that a research project undertaken by the Age Concern Institute of Gerontology is examining provision of health and social services to elderly people from black and minority ethnic groups (Tarpey, 1990).

Social services and health authority policy and practice often ignore the needs of people from black minorities and few authorities have made any systematic attempt to consider the implications of race in the delivery of services (Brent Community Health Council, 1981; Torkington, 1983; Donovan, 1984; Mares et al., 1985; Roys, 1988; Townsend and Etherington, 1988; Glendenning and Pearson, 1988; Pearson, 1988; McNaught, 1988; Commission for Racial Equality, 1989a; Connelly, 1989; Naina Patel, 1990, Eribo, 1991; Bowes and Sim, 1991; Johnson, 1991; Wallace, 1991; Abiola Ogunsola, 1992). In order to understand the failure of statutory provision to achieve even the limited goal of culturally and linguistically sensitive services, it is necessary to understand the economic, social and political context in which the plurality of cultures and social service provision exists (Roys, 1988; Naina Patel, 1990). Any analysis, it is argued, has to acknowledge that racism, both individual and institutional, exists within service provision and perpetuates racial inequality (Bandana Ahmad, 1988a; Roys, 1988; Cameron et al., 1989a).

Racism can be conscious or unconscious, operating at both an individual and institutional level. As defined in the introduction, individual racism occurs when a white person treats a black person unfairly because of his/her racial or ethnic origins; institutional racism is embedded in the operational practices of an organisation. Health and social services, therefore, need to question not only how individual practitioners relate to their black clients but also how the priorities and policies of institutions are decided, by whom and in whose interests. This chapter examines institutional and individual racism: first, by describing the effect that assumptions of cultural diversity have had on policy and practice, and secondly, by exploring the policy and practice of social service departments (SSDs) and health authorities, in relation to people who form black minorities.

## The idea of cultural diversity

The ideology of cultural diversity continues to dominate policy and practice. This view purports that diversity in language, religion, cultural norms and expectations prevents effective communication and creates misunderstanding between the majority and distinct minorities. Overcoming the linguistic and cultural barriers which cause misunderstanding, therefore, should result in more sensitive and responsive services (Ballard, 1989).

Bandana Ahmad (1988a) points out that the commitment to the idea of cultural diversity is evident in the emergence of packages aimed to inform social work professionals about the culture of their black clients. A consequence of these packages, however, is an inadequate conceptualisation of black culture, grounded in inappropriate generalisations (Atkin, 1991a). By providing over-generalised mechanical summaries of key cultural characteristics there is a dual danger both of assuming that this knowledge somehow solves the 'problem' and of perpetuating and reinforcing cultural stereotypes and myths. Durrant (1989), for example, argued that few people would attempt to sum up in a single sentence the European approach to child-rearing; 'simplistic and insulting' stereotypes should not therefore be applied to black people. Such an approach denies individuality and fails to recognise that the process of migration and the emergence of a black British generation will subtly remould the cultural norms of any community. Consequently the process of cultural enlightenment among social service practitioners can often reinforce their prejudices and narrow their perspectives with cultural stereotypes (Dominelli, 1988; Pearson, 1988; Bandana Ahmad, 1988a; Jervis, 1990).

Many researchers document the danger of negative stereotypes. Old adages, assumptions and cultural misrepresentation can deny services to black people when they are at their most vulnerable. Local authorities, for example, often list black older people as 'high risk' clients, 'closed cases' because of 'non-co-operation', 'difficult to work with', or 'family caring' (Williams, 1988). Evers *et al.* (1989) identified two stereotypes and myths which characterise the practice of service providers. These included the view that black people are to blame for their own needs because of deviant and 'unsatisfactory' lifestyles; or are not in need of help because of their family and community support networks.

The assumption that Asian people live in self-supporting families is a particularly serious myth, often used as an excuse for not making necessary changes to the existing services and expanding the level of service provision to black minorities (Pearson, 1988; Atkin *et al.*, 1989a; Naina Patel, 1990). The general belief that the extended family has the material and emotional resources to meet the needs of family members and that intervention or support from social services is not required, can lead to neglect by default (Connelly, 1988a). Another myth concerns language. Service practitioners often see language as the principal barrier to effective service provision. An adequate supply of interpreters and leaflets in appropriate languages would therefore, 'solve' the problem. Language differences are, of course, crucial and pose a barrier to service receipt, but as argued earlier, communication consists of more than language skills and literacy (Pearson, 1988; Atkin *et al.*, 1989a).

Approaches which emphasise cultural diversity can result in a preoccupation with the cultural practices of black people (Pearson, 1983b; Dominelli, 1988; Rocheron, 1988; Atkin, 1991a; Rhodes, 1991). Ahmad *et al.* (1989) for example, argued that health education is essentially about culture and victim blaming, without giving due reference to the social circumstances of individuals. The work of Foster (1988), who studied health visitors' perspectives on working in a multi-ethnic society, confirmed this. Health visitors, she argues, identified cultural differences and language as major issues, but ignored the structural disadvantage faced by black people.

Williams (1988), in describing black people's experience of social services, described the 'scant recognition' of racism. Many argue black people are over represented in aspects of social services activity which involve overt social control and institutionalization (Williams, 1988; Roys, 1988; Dominelli, 1989a; Lunn, 1989). Several authors, for example, have noted the over-representation of black people in psychiatric institutions (Mercer, 1984; Tonkin, 1987; Jenkinson, 1988; Ambreen Hameed, 1989). Josie Durrant (cited by Lunn, 1989), former assistant director of Lambeth Social Service Department, said:

> If you look at the high numbers of black children in care, and the numbers of black youths in detention centres, it is clear that all the

controlling parts of social work have had a detrimental effect on black people. But with the optional parts, like day centres for elderly people, black people haven't had a look in.

As a result black clients' experiences of service provision often leave them angry and estranged. Moreover black users often characterise SSDs as being difficult to communicate with, slow to respond, unwilling to understand, narrow in perspective, resistant to pressure and slow to change (Hughes and Reba Bhaduri, 1987; Williams, 1988; Jowell et al., 1990).

## Social services: policy and practice

Writing in 1978, an Association of Directors of Social Services/ Commission for Racial Equality (ADSS/CRE) working group concluded that the response of social services departments to the existence of multi-racial communities had been 'patchy, piecemeal and lacking in strategy'. Subsequent research over a number of years has shown a continued lack of attention to the delivery of appropriate and adequate services to black and ethnic minorities. A study of service provision for ethnic minorities in Britain and the USA, for example, criticised British social services departments for a 'muddle of principles' and a reluctance to 'experiment and [engage in] practical action' (Cheetham, 1981). In 1982, The British Association of Social Work published guidelines for working in a multi-cultural society, in which it argued the inadequacy of the 'colour-blind' approach which many SSDs adopted to service provision for ethnic minorities.

Eight years on, Scott (1988) similarly outlined the failure of SSDs to provide culturally appropriate services for ethnic minority users. First, he argued, SSDs fail to advertise clearly what services are on offer. This is a problem for all potential users, black or white, but particularly so for people who have less contact with the traditional ways of picking up information, such as local papers, and even more so for those who do not speak English as their first language. Secondly, Scott suggested that members of ethnic minority populations were further discouraged from contact with departments because they felt that services were not provided with their needs in mind. Scott concluded that most departments offered a 'take-it-or-leave-it' service, provided without detailed knowledge of, or consultation with, local people. The lack of take-up of many services by black people, he suggested, is used to justify the failure to prioritise the needs of ethnic minorities and to prove there is no point in developing different provision thereby sustaining the self-fulfilling prophecy.

The under-representation of black older people in receipt of the home help service in Liverpool led Rooney (1987) to conclude:

Racism and incompetence combined to subvert the potential of the scheme but they were legitimised within an organisational culture which wrote its own rules as it went along, and bound those who were of the organisation in its complicity.

Three years later a conference of Asian social workers suggested that many Asians contact social services departments only in 'the most desperate of circumstances' because of their negative experience of white institutions (Holmes, 1990). Don Naik, in describing how social services fail Britain's Asians, concluded that 'a picture is painted of neglect, bigotry and lazy thinking' (Holmes, 1990).

## Equal opportunity policies

The difficulties faced by SSDs have led many to implement equal opportunity policies. These policies have been the subject of extensive empirical investigation (Townsend and Etherington, 1988; Social Services Inspectorate cited in Pearson, 1988; Commission for Racial Equality, 1989a; Reba Bhaduri and Wright, 1990; Bowes and Sim, 1991). Two reports, in particular, provide detailed information. First, the Commission for Racial Equality (CRE) carried out a detailed survey as a follow-up to the 1978 Association of Directors of Social Services/ Commission for Racial Equality working group report on service provision to ethnic minorities (1989a). The 1989 survey targeted 116 departments in England, Scotland and Wales. The departments were mostly in areas of high ethnic minority population and, of the 116 selected, 70 responded. Secondly, Pearson (1988) summarised a series of inspections carried out by four regional teams of the Social Services Inspectorate (SSI) between 1986–1988. SSI reports submitted by four regional teams document these findings: North West (Hughes, 1986; Hughes and Reba Bhaduri, 1987); West Midlands (Cypher, 1988); London (Prime, 1987); and Yorkshire and Humberside (Whitfield, 1990).

Pearson's report revealed that most SSDs visited during SSI visits had no policy for responding to the needs of the multi-racial population (Pearson, 1988); two-thirds of the departments responding to the CRE survey did not have a written equal opportunities policy and 13 departments did not intend to introduce one. Even among those departments which had committed themselves to promoting equal opportunity in service provision, policy implementation was still in its early stages (Commission for Racial Equality, 1989a). Moreover Hughes and Reba Bhaduri's inspection of 17 local authorities in the North West in 1985–86 showed that while 12 local authorities had an equal opportunities policy in place, its effect on social services delivery was undetectable (Hughes and Reba Bhaduri, 1987 and 1990). Although inspectors anticipated engaging with managers on problems of implementation, interviews dealt mostly with the need for policy in the first place. Few departments had made much progress with services for black and ethnic minority communities. The projects that existed operated on the fringe of mainstream provision, financed either by Section 11 monies[3] or from urban programme grants. The CRE (1989a) report confirmed this:

> Ten years on from the ADSS/CRE report, most departments still have ad hoc arrangements without a wider strategy for ensuring equal opportunity provision across the whole range of services.

## Social work

Social work practice further illustrates the direct and indirect discrimination faced by black people. The literature, although identifying examples of good practice, suggests that many social workers operate in a racist manner (Hughes and Reba Bhaduri, 1987; Halahmy, 1988; Fry, 1989; Huby and Salkind, 1990). Social workers either over-emphasise cultural differences or totally ignore race and culture as relevant factors in the case. As a result assessments can be judgmental, patronising and stereotypical (Hughes and Reba Bhaduri, 1987). The same report quoted social workers who spoke of their unwillingness to intrude, and of their anxieties about offending against cultural mores or of appearing racist. In general social workers said they felt de-skilled and recognised that the service offered was, often, of poorer quality than white clients might receive in the same circumstances. Hughes and Reba Bhaduri (1987) concluded:

> Whatever the pattern of practice by individual social workers, the organisational and operational context had a profound effect on their performance. For example, good practice by individuals was camou-flaged when their employing agency failed to win the trust and confidence of black and minority ethnic communities.

Overall, Hughes and Reba Bhaduri (1987) argued, it was apparent that a lack of appropriate training and ethnically-sensitive supervision, and an absence of management back-up left social service staff ill-equipped to deal with the challenge of working in a multi-racial community.

## Health authorities: policy and practice

In 1987 the Department of Health organised a National Health Service management seminar on ethnic minority health. Thirty-five district health authorities as well as chair persons of regional health authorities attended the seminar. The then Health Minister, Tony Newton, outlined several ways in which health authorities could improve their

---

[3] Section 11 of the 1966 Local Government Act encourages local authorities to employ extra staff to help 'commonwealth immigrants' whose language or culture differs from the rest of the community.

provision to black and ethnic minorities. These included allocating specific responsibility for developing services to a designated officer, drawing up district plans of action, and collaborating with other organisations such as social service departments and family practitioner committees, where joint action was necessary.

In the past, the Department of Health has issued a series of circulars concerning the issue of race. The circulars, however, seem to have little impact on the practice of health authorities and family practitioner committees/family health service authorities (Baxter, 1987; McNaught, 1988). One notable exception was Derbyshire FPC's response to a 1987 circular, which addressed concerns about 'obstacles to equal access to health services which ethnic minorities may face as a result of linguistic and cultural differences'. In response, Derbyshire FPC conducted a review of service provision for the ethnic minorities (Cassidy and Worrall, 1988). In general, however, McNaught (1988) noted that the range of recommendations issued by the Department of Health and health authorities is limited and characterised by an uncertainty about what should be done. As a result policy concerns have not been translated into practice.

## Equal opportunity policies

Health authorities seem reluctant to implement equal opportunities policies (Connelly, 1989). For this reason the King's Fund established an equal opportunities task force in 1986. The task force aimed to help health authorities tackle racial discrimination in employment practice and service provision (Ellis, 1990) and has issued publications about the implementation of equal opportunities policies, including a model equal opportunities policy, ethnic monitoring, making the best use of equal opportunities committees, and the work of expert advisers. These have been circulated to all health authorities. Other projects include exploring management recruitment, procedures for hospital medical appointments, a survey of ethnic minority representation among health authority members and racial equality in the nursing profession.

Since its establishment, the task force has witnessed a change of attitude to equal opportunities policies among many health authorities with an increasing realization that what was regarded as an optional extra is, in the 1990s, an essential component of efficient personnel practice and good management (Ellis, 1990). However, although the task force recognises that some health authorities have adopted models of good practice, the overall conclusion is more pessimistic. Most authorities, although committing themselves to an equal opportunities policy as a statement of intent, often do not follow this up with a programme of action or an allocation of the responsibilities and resources necessary to ensure that real movement takes place. The task force recommends that implementing equal opportunities policies should be a formal objective laid down by the NHS Management Executive, with targets set and achievement evaluated.

## Racism and health service provision

The problems faced by the health service in meeting the needs of black communities, although similar in character to those found in social service departments, seem even greater. There is growing recognition and acceptance, both nationally and within local health authorities, that the health service does not meet the needs of Britain's black and ethnic minorities (Glendenning and Pearson, 1988; McNaught, 1988; Johnson, 1991). Health authorities are said often to accord people from ethnic minorities low priority and to be resistant to placing racial discrimination on the policy agenda (Hicks, 1988b; McNaught, 1988).

Although there has been no systematic study of the character or extent of racial discrimination in the NHS, the literature documenting ethnic minority people's experience of health services identifies racism as a major feature (Brent Community Health Council, 1981; Torkington 1983; Donovan, 1984; Mares et al., 1985; Glendenning and Pearson, 1988; McNaught, 1988; Shah Ebrahim, 1990). McNaught (1988) commented that many of these problems are not specific to ethnic minorities, with the NHS having a poor record for 'user friendliness'. What distinguishes poor treatment for minorities, he argued, is that they seem to receive it because of their racial, cultural or ethnic origin, as opposed to other personal characteristics. Similarly Ahmad (1989) argues that racism within the NHS affects virtually all black people, with common stereotypes portraying black people as calling out doctors unnecessarily, or being trivial complainers, and time wasters.

Two reports highlight the failure of health services to provide appropriate services for black and ethnic minorities as a result of racism – the first by Glendenning and Pearson (1988) and the second by The National Association of Health Authorities (NAHA) working party for health services for black and minority ethnic groups (NAHA, 1988).

Glendenning and Pearson (1988) reviewed the organisation and delivery of health services to black and ethnic minorities and concluded that institutional and individual racism persist at every level of the organisation. They argue that health services do not seem to consider difference and diversity, and assume their policies, procedures and practices are equally appropriate for everyone. This results in unfavourable treatment and unequal access for black and ethnic minority people. The authors concluded that black people are regarded as 'abnormal', and outside 'normal' British experience. Consequently any change in health authority policy or practice becomes a 'special concession', rather than a late and justified response towards providing an appropriate service.

The NAHA working party report on health services for black and minority ethnic groups described the extent of racism within the National Health Service. In particular it emphasised inconsistent standards of care, lack of integral planning, limited NHS response to health issues which particularly affect black and ethnic minority groups, and the failure of most health authorities to implement comprehensive equal opportunities policies with monitoring, evaluation and review processes (NAHA, 1988). The report concluded:

> The NHS must acknowledge the existence of institutional and individual racism and realise that widespread racial discrimination occurs in both employment practices and service provision.

NAHA's report, however, met with a mixed response. An editorial in Health Services Management Journal (Anon, 1989b), although accepting that individual, cultural and institutional racial discrimination existed within the NHS, said that the NAHA report had not discovered a new problem or produced new solutions. By contrast, Conroy and Safder Mohammed (1989) argue that, although the NAHA report acknowledged that racism is embedded in the organisational culture of the NHS, it under-estimated the problem. A fundamental weakness of the report, they suggested, is the failure to comprehend the effect of institutional racism. By failing to be critical of existing projects, and lacking any framework for assessment, the report is therefore unconvincing and does not recognise that little or nothing of lasting effect can be done without financial resources. The authors viewed with particular scepticism the suggestion, by NAHA and ministers, that progress would be monitored and maintained by the regional health authorities through the regional review system. Conroy and Safder Mohammed (1989) concluded with a 'plea' for a more 'thoughtful, comprehensive and properly resourced and committed activity in the field of race equality'.

Three empirical examples – mental health, the practice of general practitioners and community nurses – are used here to further illustrate the racism faced by black people in the receipt of community health services.

## Mental health
Racism appears particularly evident in black people's experience of mental health services (Mercer, 1984; Tonkin, 1987; Grimsley and Ashok Bhat, 1988; Jenkinson, 1988; Ambreen Hameed, 1989; Anuradha Sayal, 1990; Francis, 1990; Nalini Sadhoo, 1990; Bowl and Barnes, 1991; Knowles, 1991). This includes both treatment and diagnosis.

Racism, for example, is apparent in the diagnosis of mental disorder and permeates the professions empowered to define and control it (Tonkin, 1987). Grimsley and Ashok Bhat (1988) argued that there was no simple explanation for differences in the prevalence of mental illness among different ethnic groups. They pointed out that Britain's black population was more likely to be admitted to hospital on a compulsory basis, and therefore more likely to have experienced police and social work involvement. Once admitted, black people were more likely to receive a diagnosis of psychosis. Moreover, the little available evidence on treatment shows that black people tend to be on harsher forms of medication than equivalent white groups as well as viewed differently once in hospital (Grimsley and Ashok Bhat, 1988). Ambreen Hameed (1989) examined the over-representation of black people, and more especially of young black men, in psychiatric institutions and identified the importance of stereotypes held by psychiatric staff in explaining this. William Bingley, former Legal Director of MIND (cited Ambreen Hameed, 1989) believed:

> There is considerable evidence for the existence of stereotypes among psychiatric staff. From perusing medical reports, the impression I get is that black people are described much more than whites in terms of potential violence.

Aggrey Burke, a consultant psychiatrist, made a similar observation (cited Tonkin, 1987). He argued that psychiatric reports show 'an obsession' with ideas of black people being bad. To overcome these problems Burke incorporated an anti-racist perspective into his dealings both with clients and with staff engaged in training for the mental health professions. Tonkin (1987), however, sees these initiatives as isolated and concluded:

> Sensitive mental health care for minorities means, in other words, much what it means for anyone else. Marked with the twin brands of racial prejudice and mental illness, black people may still have to travel a longer and harder route to find it.

### General practice
General practice also provides examples of individual racism (Jarman, 1983; Pearson, 1986; Glendenning and Pearson, 1988; McNaught, 1990; Wallace, 1991). Smith and Stiff's (1985) report on general practice in North West London, for example, categorised black minorities as the 'main problem' for general practice in the area. Wright (1983) undertook a study examining 39 general practitioners' perceptions of their Asian patients and concluded that his overwhelming impression was of general practitioners not only puzzled by the influx of Asians to their practices, but also aware of considerable problems of management, yet unable or unwilling to adjust.

Although as mentioned earlier Asian patients frequently choose to register with doctors of Asian origin, this does not necessarily solve 'the problem'. Black general practitioners are subject to the same professional norms, training, policies, practices and role models as their white colleagues. Ahmad (1989) commented that discrimination was not confined to white health professionals and argued that some Asian doctors are equally guilty of holding prejudiced views, based on racial stereotypes. Shabira Moledina (1988) reported that Asian older people complain that Asian general practitioners have become too 'westernized', and as a result fail to take complaints from Asian patients seriously. Moreover, although linguistic barriers between the doctor and patient were not present, there were others of class and status.

## Community nursing

Cameron et al. (1989b) highlighted the under-representation of black older and disabled people on district nursing caseloads. Their material showed that district nurses tended to adhere to myths and stereotypes about black older people, such as, as we have seen, 'they look after their own'. These views of black people also had implications for patient care. Some nurses, for example, subscribed to the belief that cultural factors foster dependence and low compliance with treatment regimes. The nurses saw this as undesirable, conflicting with the way in which they wanted patients to respond. Consequently community nurses saw black people as a problem.

Badger et al. (1988) suggested that nurses tended to assume homogeneity among their black clients. They concluded that without more enlightened information, it is all too easy for nurses to look to culture for explanation and legitimation in relation to their perspectives on black patients, with their understanding of black people's culture shaped largely by the partial and limited awareness held by society.

Foster (1988), who examined the perspectives of 48 health visitors working in a multi-ethnic community, highlighted the practice of individual racism among community nurses. Comments made by health visitors included the suggestion that minority groups should give up their culture. One health visitor stated this view particularly strongly, arguing that black and ethnic minorities should conform to British society. Health visitors saw black patients as 'problems' and only two health visitors stressed the enjoyment which they gained from working in a multi-ethnic society.

Most health visitors, however, did not identify racism as a problem in their practice:

> I never think of colour, in fact when I was a nurse and had worked with other black nurses it never occurred to me that they had a

different colour from mine, so I think it's really made bigger than it is. To me there's no such thing as someone having black or red skin. To me it's no issue at all.

The eight health visitors who believed racism was a major issue suggested it was difficult for health visitors to avoid holding negative stereotypes or patronising their patients. One health visitor said:

I'm sure I find myself shouting at people who don't speak English and doing the typical things that you do to people who don't understand English and I'm sure, sometimes you think, 'Oh God, why do they do that'. Which you might not think of from somebody from your own culture. I mean I can honestly say that I try not to let it affect the way I deliver my services, but I think if somebody assessed me they would probably pick out glaring faults that I'm totally unaware of really.

Foster (1988) concluded that the practice of health visitors tended to explain the behaviour of black and ethnic minority clients in terms of a 'different and problematic culture' and the unequal relationship between the health visitor and patient compounded this.

## Conclusions

Few local and health authorities make any systematic attempt to consider the implications of race in service delivery. The literature highlights the direct and indirect discrimination resulting from policies, procedures and practices adopted by statutory service provision. Individual and institutional racism are fundamental in understanding this. Consequently the needs of black and ethnic minority people are not met.

# Employment, ethnic monitoring and interpreting services: a partial response

Wide-ranging recommendations arise from the critiques outlined in the previous chapter. The CRE report, for example, made four specific recommendations: first, that social services departments need to review their present policies to ensure they take into account race issues; secondly, that they need to adopt, implement and monitor a written equal opportunities policy for which senior management is directly responsible; thirdly, that they need to engage in regular consultation with ethnic minority communities to establish service areas of greatest priority; and finally, that they need to monitor the ethnic origins of service users (Commission for Racial Equality 1989a). In general, statutory services adopt a more narrowly defined response to these problems and tend to see their difficulties in developing accessible and appropriate provision to black people in terms of employment practice, interpreting services and ethnic monitoring (Commission for Racial Equality, 1989a).

Although these approaches represent a partial response the literature is almost exclusively concerned with them and therefore they form the subject of this chapter. The next chapter discusses the general limitations of these approaches.

## Employment

There are no national figures which show the numbers and positions of black and ethnic minority people working in health and social services, but local studies have shown them to be under-represented (Doyal *et al.*, 1980; Torkington, 1983; Hicks, 1988b; Commission for Racial Equality, 1989a; Hughes and Reba Bhaduri, 1990). When they are employed, black people tend to be over-represented in low status work and specialities and under-represented in high status and managerial roles (Pearson, 1988; Dominelli, 1989a; Mallinson and Best, 1990). Baxter *et al.* (1990) suggested that this is caused by racial discrimination and concluded that community services need to adopt strategies that allow the employment of people from black and ethnic minorities.

The literature establishes the need for health and social services departments to reflect the multi-cultural nature of the community served (Pearson, 1988). The 1976 Race Relations Act enables employers to seek and encourage applicants for jobs from black and ethnic minority communities and employing black workers does seem to enhance an organisation's capacity to provide services that are sensitive to differences in race and culture (Pearson, 1988; Baxter *et al.*, 1990; Mallinson and Best, 1990).

The employment of people from black and ethnic minorities does not, however, solve 'the problem' of developing a multi-racial service. Stubbs (1985) for instance, pointed to the problems of tokenism. Employing black people often comes to be seen as an end in itself, divorced from the delivery and organisation of services (Neate, 1989). Baxter *et al.* (1990) argued, for example, that black employees working with people with learning difficulties often faced the problem of supporting black clients with inappropriate services. Further, black and ethnic minority staff will experience the same training, professional norms, policies, practices and role models as their white colleagues. Therefore, black workers will not necessarily have the skills and confidence to work from an anti-racist and multi-cultural perspective (Baxter *et al.*, 1990).

Black workers often face tensions by having to chose between being loyal to the agencies that employ them or becoming advocates for their clients (Bandana Ahmad, 1988b; Owusu-Bempah, 1990). Durrant (1989) argued that:

> Black staff appear to be recruited to resolve all the dilemmas concerning race, which the organisation helped to create but cannot deal with; to act as a buffer between the black community and senior management; to initiate and provide ethnically sensitive services; to train up senior and better paid colleagues; to join every working party in the department while also doing their own job.

Roach (1989) echoed this and pointed out that, although recruiting black workers is seen as a necessary strategy to eliminate racial inequality in employment and enhance service delivery, service managers rarely discuss this with the black worker. As a result black workers often feel frustrated and exploited. Len Dimsdale, a senior manager in a London borough argued:

> White people must take responsibility. Equal opportunity policies which just bring black people into authorities put all the onus on them – the minority – to change the whole organisation. In any argument over equal rights, there's polarisation. We end up in

conflict, but as long as white people see it as our problem, we can't move forward. Equal opportunities policies often just take that conflict, which has existed for hundreds of years, internalise it, and let it play out just as it always has, with no progress.

The fundamental problem facing statutory services is perhaps the organizational climate which perceives race as a black responsibility and not as a white one. Consequently race remains a separate issue, removed from mainstream service provision, rather than being a fully integrated issue which does not require special solutions (Durrant, 1989).

## Social service departments

Many social service agencies do employ black and ethnic minority staff to make services more accessible to black communities (Sugden, 1988; Connelly, 1989; Baxter et al., 1990; Mallinson and Best, 1990) and the literature describes various initiatives (Rooney, 1987; Hardingham, 1988; Wilson, 1989; Beaver et al., 1989; Renshaw, 1989; London Borough of Camden, 1990; Poonia and Ward, 1990). A Social Services Inspectorate survey in Kirklees illustrated the importance of employing black and ethnic minority staff (Dearnley and Milner, 1986). The survey covered three areas, Batley, Fartown and Dewsbury. In Batley, where there was a social work team with Asian staff, an estimated 17 per cent of the total clients referred were Asian. (Asian people comprised 11 per cent of Batley's population.) In Dewsbury, which had no Asian social workers but where a similar proportion of the population were Asian people, only three per cent of the total clients referred to the social work department were Asian.

Discussions with social service staff, initiated by the Inspectorate, identified four problems:

- services often undervalue the particular perspectives, experiences and skills of black and ethnic minority staff;

- black staff become known as the 'race experts' which relieves white staff of their moral and professional responsibilities in this domain;

- black staff often feel restricted to 'ethnic minority' work and prevented from using their full range of professional skills. This limits their future promotion and job opportunities;

- some initiatives and methods which black people and ethnic minority staff develop as more relevant and useful approaches, can be seen as unprofessional by their colleagues and managers.

These problems often become compounded for specialist workers as many feel their ethnic origin is the only thing they can contribute to the service (Baxter et al., 1990). Other difficulties for specialist workers include unclear job descriptions, inadequate training, poor salary scales, no career structure, and no access to decision making. These difficulties contribute to low morale (Baxter et al., 1990). Further, reliance on specialist workers can have substantial drawbacks for service users (Roys, 1988). Such posts, although helping to increase the sensitivity of social services departments to the needs of minority communities, carry the danger that work with minority communities can become marginalized. Rather than methodically examining the scope and relevance of mainstream provision, authorities may define work with such communities as a specialism undertaken by relatively few, junior, specialist workers. The authority can satisfy itself and potential critics that it is attending to the needs of minority communities, when, in fact, Roys (1988) argued, no attempt has been made to evaluate their needs.

Marginalising service provision for black people is a problem identified by other writers (Cypher, 1988). Pearson (1988) noted that efforts to address the particular needs of black and minority ethnic communities are largely funded by special arrangements, and not within the mainstream of social service budgets. This can result in marginalising both the needs and the staff seeking to meet them. Social workers appointed to Section 11 posts, for example, appear to face unreasonable and unrealistic expectations, occupying an uncomfortable position between minority communities and insensitive services and an unresponsive institution (Roys, 1988; Cross et al., 1988).

## Health services

Health services appear reluctant to recognise the implications of equal opportunities in employment practice. McNaught (1988) argues:

> Some seven or eight years after the issue of HC(78)36, on equal opportunities in NHS employment, health authorities are only now treating equal opportunities as a serious issue. However progress has been slow and extremely patchy.

A report on the development of equal opportunities policies with regard to employment among London's Health Authorities, elicited responses from 31 of the 37 district health authorities and three out of the four regional health authorities (GLARE, 1987). This report concluded that equal employment opportunity within the National Health Service was in 'a critical condition'. None of the regional health authorities and only five of the district health authorities were at that time attempting to introduce programmes recommended by the Commission for Racial Equality code of practice. Of the others, some had draft programmes of action on the drawing board, some had only bare statements of intent, and six had not even reached the stage of agreeing such a statement. A second report followed which examined the progress made by health authorities in adopting equal opportunity policies which concluded there had been little progress (Safder Mohammed, 1987). Only a small number of authorities were implementing equal opportunity programmes. Many more London health authorities, at earlier stages of commitment and decision taking, were moving more hesitantly. A substantial minority, the report argues, showed few signs of movement at all, and were unlikely to consider equal opportunity policies in 'the near future'. The situation does not seem to have altered much since then (Abiola Ogunsola, 1992).

The employment of black people by health authorities, however, does not guarantee a service sensitive to cultural differences. First, as in social services, many find that their particular perspectives, experiences and skills are undervalued, and that they are not in a position of power to make decisions within the service (Baxter, 1989b). One Asian health visitor commented:

> I speak four Asian languages and thought this would be useful to the community. I applied four times to be a health visitor and was refused. Each time they told me to go and improve my English.

Another Asian health visitor said:

> I work in an area with a lot of Asian families. I speak all the languages and try to give a good service to my clients. The nursing officer told me not to spend so much time with them. I should just do practical things such as child development assessment and immunization. She said that is the job I am paid to do. (Baxter, 1989b)

Secondly, the posts of black workers are often not funded from main revenue budgets but from a mixture of 'soft money' from local authorities, Inner Cities Partnership, the Manpower Services Commission, charities and the major voluntary organisations (McNaught, 1988). This further marginalises the position of black workers. Shushilla Patel (Millar, 1990) recommends that health authorities should fund future initiatives from mainstream funding.

## Ethnic monitoring

Several reports raise the need for ethnic monitoring (Townsend and Etherington, 1988; Pearson, 1988; Commission for Racial Equality 1989a; Abiola Ogunsola, 1992). The CRE, for example, regard ethnic monitoring as central in implementing race equality strategies of the future (Commission for Racial Equality, 1989a). From this viewpoint, collecting data is seen as a valuable instrument for change, providing information that can be used to promote racial justice and equality of opportunity, and encourage both central and local government to implement relevant policies. If race equality programmes are to redress under-representation among black and ethnic minorities in employment, as well as tackle unavailable and inappropriate service provision, outcomes must be measured and accounted for (Connelly, 1988b; Commission for Racial Equality, 1989a; Wilson and McGloin, 1989; Bandana Ahmad, 1989b; Jabeer Butt et al., 1991). In this respect the decision by the Department of Health to introduce in-patient ethnic monitoring by April 1993 is an encouraging development. This will generate information on the use of services by different ethnic groups, thereby highlighting deficiencies in provision (Veena Soni Raleigh, 1992). However, while there is a need for ethnic monitoring there are also 'certain dangers' (Bandana Ahmad, 1989b; Jabeer Butt et al., 1991). These include misuse of the information collected, use of monitoring as a device for delaying any real change, and the risk of avoiding essential dialogue between service users and managers.

The literature documents the problems local authorities face in ethnic monitoring. The CRE report (1989a) found that of the 18 SSDs who had adopted ethnic monitoring, 12 reported difficulties. Seven replied that staff were reluctant to collect ethnic origin data because of client suspicions about how such information might be used. Four departments said that staff were uncertain how to explain the categories to clients, either because of disagreements over the categories used, or because of the lack of appropriate training. One response suggested that problems occurred because of a lack of commitment by staff and management to the forceful pursuit of an equal opportunities policy. Few authorities have adopted specialist record keeping for ethnic minorities, either in terms of service receipt or employment (Townsend and Etherington, 1988). The reasons given by authorities for not doing so included: 'bureaucratic'; 'big job'; 'dearth of experience about how to do it and how to use results'; and 'staff reluctance to take part'. Townsend and Etherington (1988) concluded that even local authorities who kept records found it difficult to produce actual figures. They suggested that given the failure to produce adequate data one must question the quality of much of the current record keeping. Similarly Wilson and McGloin (1989) suggested that ethnic monitoring is not taken seriously by many authorities.

Health services appear rarely to consider the issue of ethnic monitoring. West Lambeth Health Authority's Equal Opportunities Officer summed up the problem:

> The main difficulty with implementing equal opportunities is getting managers to admit their is a problem. They tend to go about denying that racism exists. (cited, Daloni Carlisle, 1990)

In this respect, health authorities are lagging behind developments taking place in social services, who, as we have seen, are more likely to recognise the need for ethnic monitoring.

## Interpreting services

Language is a known barrier to service receipt and the effective use of social and health services requires knowledge of services as well as necessary linguistic skills. Material concerned with implementing the NHS and Community Care Act identifies the importance of providing interpreters.

One example the literature explores is how language problems can prevent an effective general practitioner intervention. Wright (1983) speculated that the dismissal by GPs of 'trivial complaints' may include ailments that patients cannot explain because of the language barrier. The doctor, therefore, is unlikely to diagnose and appropriately manage these complaints. Language barriers also mean that the content of advice and guidance on critical matters such as compliance with drug regimes may be ineffective (Shabira Moledina, 1988; McNaught, 1990). Norman (1985) quoted a Birmingham study which found that illiteracy and poor comprehension of English, as well as unfamiliarity with western medicine, led to misuse of medication among Asian patients. Personal counselling of patients in their first language by a skilled pharmacist, and full instruction leaflets improve the situation.

It is necessary, therefore, for health and social services to have an effective strategy for dealing with this difficulty (Pearson, 1988). In most situations it is inappropriate to rely on ad hoc use of relatives or friends to act as interpreters, particularly when confidential information is discussed. Furthermore the informal use of members of staff with relevant language skills to interpret for colleagues is often perceived by them as exploitation. Staff and communities need access to professional interpreters who have an adequate understanding of the operation and delivery of the health and social services. Translation of publicity material and advisory leaflets into appropriate languages for the community concerned seems essential (Pearson, 1988; Brotchie, 1989).

The failure of services to develop such a strategy is well documented (Shackman, 1983, cited in Brotchie, 1989; Zahida Hussain, Saunders and Baker, forthcoming, cited in Brotchie, 1989; Fewster, 1989; McHanwell, 1989; Cole, 1990; Jackson, 1990). There appears a particular reluctance among health authorities to employ interpreters (Fewster, 1989) and white health professionals often believe that Asian people do not make any attempt to learn English (Badger et al., 1988; Foster, 1988; Ahmad, 1989). Ahmad (1989) for example, quoted a response to a paper on bilingual consultation in the The Lancet:

> Patients from ethnic minority communities should recognise that it is in their interest to be familiar and comfortable with the language of the land.

Ahmad, however, suggested that limited proficiency in English should not be a barrier to service provision. Health authorities, he suggested, must appreciate that equitable provision of services is their responsibility irrespective of the patients' linguistic and cultural background, sex or physical ability.

## Conclusions

The recommendations of reports which are critical of service delivery to black and ethnic minorities, although wide ranging, seem to have had limited impact on service provision. Three prominent themes – the employment of staff from black and ethnic minorities, the use of interpreters, and ethnic monitoring – reflect how statutory services address the issue.

The need for health and social services to reflect the multi-racial nature of the communities they service is well established. Employing people from black and ethnic minorities does not, however, solve the problem of developing a multi-racial service. The organisational climate that perceives race primarily as a black responsibility and not as a white one is perhaps the fundamental problem facing statutory services.

A number of reports raise the need for ethnic monitoring as a means of evaluating those strategies aimed at addressing past imbalances of black under-representation in employment, as well as inappropriate services for black people. Problems about this approach include: anxieties about possible misuse of the information collected; use of monitoring as a device for delaying any real change; and the risk of avoiding essential dialogue between service users and service practitioners.

Language is a known barrier to service receipt and it is therefore essential for health and social services to develop an effective strategy for dealing with this difficulty. The literature, however, documents the failure of services, by and large, to develop such a strategy.

# CHAPTER SIX

# A way forward for statutory policy and practice

The previous chapters demonstrate the partial response adopted by statutory services to meet the needs of black and ethnic minority communities. Providing appropriate and accessible services to people from black and ethnic minorities, however, requires more than this. This chapter examines the potential for development of policy and practice in the future and illustrates the limitations of this partial response by placing the debate in a wider context. Understanding how institutional racism, in its various guises, operates is essential in ensuring effective policy and practice for the future.

## Social service departments

Many local authorities are becoming aware of the potential significance of race and ethnicity in formulating policy (Pearson, 1988; Arshi Ahmad, 1990; Reba Bhaduri and Wright, 1990; Naina Patel, 1990). Connelly (1989) examined the changes taking place within social services departments during the 1980s. Although acknowledging that such change may be invisible to black and white staff, and to those in local black communities hoping for a reduction of barriers and increased access to services, she identified four major changes. First, during the early 1980s, the subject of race equality was, when it arose at all, usually discussed in general terms, or else in relation to individual cases. Now race issues have a higher profile with discussion of the race aspects of the work of a department likely to be more frequent, more detailed but also more contentious. The greater openness of discussion reveals a wide range of views. Secondly, social service departments are more likely to acknowledge that the issues are about 'us' (the department) and not just 'them' (the local black populations or service users). Thirdly, service practitioners recognise that black people are participants in the situation and not merely passive recipients of whatever the department decides to offer. Finally, service managers now understand that the aim of service provision is not simply about input but about changed outcomes for the local black populations.

Other constraints on change, however, have emerged (Connelly, 1989). These include: resentment of staff; complacency about current methods of dealing with race equality; anxiety about the racism of others; game-playing, where managerial or political games use race as a counter; marginalisation of staff working with black users; and abdication of responsibility, on grounds that service provision is insufficiently pre-pared to meet the needs of black users. Although these factors present major impediments to change it would be a mistake to assume that intractable racism is always present:

> There may be genuine uncertainty or confusion, or whole-hearted concentration on another issue. Inertia, indifference, lack of infor-mation and lack of empathy all play a part. (Connelly, 1989)

Connelly also questioned the optimism that once organisations had an explicit overall policy on race equality, changes in the delivery of services would follow automatically. Although policies are necessary, they are not sufficient. It is also necessary to examine practice.

Despite a commitment to race equality, evidence suggests that racism still persists in social service departments (Pearson, 1988). Bandana Ahmad (1989b) described a situation of 'black pain, white hurt'. She argued that 'black pain' occurred because little change had been achieved. 'White hurt' occurred because, despite the adoption of anti-racist policies, there had been no change; the criticisms and dissatisfac-tion of black people still existed. Owusu-Bempah (1989a), similarly, argued that the increased interest from local authority employers in equal opportunities policies was not reflected in the experience of black people. He described a new institutional racism, where organiations are able to create an impression of commitment to racial equality while remaining fundamentally racist. Rafael Halahmy (1990), principal officer in London Borough of Brent, argued that racism was essentially a power struggle, a matter of who holds the power and whether they are willing to share it with all groups in society. The reason that progress is taking too long, he concluded, is the strength of those who resist relinquishing power.

Local authorities need to have a commitment to change. Durrant (1989), whilst not wishing to detract from individual actions, or from initiatives which some departments have attempted, argued that rac-ism and support work with black and ethnic minority families were not issues amenable to individual goodwill and solutions. Without more fundamental commitment to long-term change, the genuine attempts of many concerned and committed staff will remain frustrated, with the recipients equally frustrated and intolerant of the efforts of services. Following this, Mallinson and Best (1990) argued that equal oppor-tunities policies need implementation strategies if they are to become translated into practice. Similarly Ratna Dutt (1989b) concluded that many authorities' equal opportunities policies are 'not worth the paper they are written on', because there is no commitment to implementation.

## Health authorities

Although there is growing recognition within local health authorities that they are not meeting the needs of black and ethnic minorities (Glendenning and Pearson, 1988) few health authorities appear aware of the potential significance of race in formulating policies. Stocking (1990) argued that health authorities seem to go through two stages in meeting the needs of black and ethnic minority populations. Initially, they establish services for medical conditions affecting only minority groups; for example, sickle cell disease. Health authorities then recognise the limitations of this approach and go on to look at some of the more obvious language and cultural differences. McNaught (1988) identified a similar pattern and believed the response to be inadequate. He argued that the pattern of these initiatives suggested a concern with problems of access, rather than with the development of different approaches to service delivery. Moreover language and cultural problems received greater attention than racial discrimination.

The literature does describe several initiatives which could have a bearing on future policy and practice. In 1988 the National Association of Health Authorities (NAHA) recommended establishing a central resource unit providing information on service provision to black and ethnic minorities (NAHA, 1988). In 1991 The King's Fund Centre 'Information Exchange' project was launched. The project collects and distributes information about statutory and voluntary bodies providing health services for black and ethnic minority users.

Several authorities have also appointed race advisers (for example Newham, Ealing, Camberwell, Haringey and Liverpool). McNaught (1988) argued that, conceptually, the posts represent an acceptance of the need for internal change in the health authority's response to minority communities and health workers. Haringey was the first health authority to appoint an ethnic minorities development worker (Hicks, 1988b; Nirveen Kalsi and Constantinides, 1989). Nirveen Kalsi was appointed in 1985 to advise on both service delivery and employment. In 1986, a second adviser was appointed as equal opportunities adviser. Nirveen Kalsi, in explaining her role, said:

> Much groundwork was needed to raise awareness of race issues. In particular the developmental worker had to explain why colour blind services might not be equally accessible and acceptable to everyone and that more equitable and sensitive services would ultimately mean better services for all. (Nirveen Kalsi and Constantinides, 1989)

Consultation with comunity organisations, resulting from the project, led to identification of several priority areas such as services for older people and mental health provision. The project also introduced a link worker scheme, provided appropriate washing and bathing arrangements for ethnic minority patients in hospital, and produced translated audio-cassettes explaining service provision for those who do not read or write English.

West Lambeth Health Authority has also undertaken initiatives in this area, recruiting an outreach worker with a brief to recruit people from ethnic minorities into nursing (Carlisle, 1990). This is part of a general attempt by West Lambeth Health Authority to develop a multi-racial approach to health service provision. McNaught (1990), in evaluating the West Lambeth scheme, described similar problems to those in Haringey. While there had been considerable development in relevant policies in West Lambeth, he argues that there was a lack of 'a robust strategy' to achieve improvements. Racial prejudice and insensitivity to the socio-cultural features of the local population, he concluded, pervaded the whole organisation, even among staff in senior management and professional roles.

The West Lambeth case-study showed that, despite the existence of policy statements, there was an inability or reluctance to implement the clinical and organizational measures that would lead to an improvement in services to local ethnic minorities. McNaught (1990) concluded that personal, social and organizational factors in part accounted for this situation; but he suggests that the predominant influences seemed to have been a combination of poor management, insensitivity to ethnic minorities and their needs, and racial prejudice. This brings the argument full circle by indicating that individual and institutional racism represent a barrier to appropriate and effective service delivery for black and ethnic minorities. This is an issue taken up in the final chapter.

## Conclusions

Some local and health authorities are becoming aware of the potential significance of race and ethnicity in formulating policy. This, however, has had a limited effect on practice. Statutory provision, therefore, needs to address more fully the mechanisms that might achieve accessible and appropriate services for black and ethnic minorities, and the principles that underlie it. Understanding how individual and institutional racism operates becomes fundamental to future policy and practice.

# Voluntary provision

Many commentators over the years have advocated a partnership between the statutory and voluntary sectors in the delivery of community services (Barclay, 1982; Griffiths, 1988; Wagner, 1988). Government policy now promotes the contracting out of community provision to voluntary and private agencies. The voluntary sector, therefore, will become an increasingly important provider of community services. The relationship between black communities and the voluntary sector is central to any future research programme. This chapter examines this relationship by outlining first the knowledge and use of mainstream voluntary agencies amongst black communities, and secondly, the policy and practice of the voluntary sector.

## Knowledge and use of voluntary agencies

For black communities, the voluntary sector includes both mainstream agencies and services provided by minorities for minorities. The latter tend to be small-scale and locally based and there is little systematic information about black people's use and experience of these services. This section concentrates on the services provided by the nationally-based voluntary sector.

As is the case with statutory community service provision, few black people receive support from traditional voluntary agencies (Farrah, 1986; McCalman, 1990); and low take-up is often attributed to voluntary services' neglect of black communities' needs (Dungate, 1984). This is confirmed by the work of Field and Jackson (1989) who provide the most systematic study of Asian people's relationship to voluntary provision. Their study, carried out in 1985, interviewed 1,000 white and Gujerati Asian households in two parts of London. The survey covered most types of service provided by the voluntary sector, and included child care, care of the elderly and disabled, youth services, advice services, and participation in community groups and recreation clubs and groups. Asian voluntary groups provided only a small proportion of these services.

The results indicated a low use of services by Asians throughout a range of provision with Asian families less likely to report receiving outside voluntary help than white families (Field and Jackson, 1989).

The authors put forward four possible explanations for the low use of voluntary services by Asian people. First, voluntary organisations often assume an Asian person's needs are already met by the extended family, or by Asian religious or community groups. Secondly, Asian people were not aware of the services on offer. Thirdly, the services on offer were culturally inappropriate to Asian people. Fourthly, discrimination of various types prevented Asians from using the services on offer.

## Policy and practice

The delivery and organisation of voluntary services to black minorities provides the context within which the 'mixed economy' of service provision advocated in the Government's strategy for community care will operate. As we have said, voluntary provision for black minorities includes both mainstream agencies and services provided by minorities for minorities. To reflect this, this section is divided into two parts.

### The mainstream voluntary sector

A neglect of black communities' requirements seems to characterise the mainstream voluntary sector (Shabira Moledina, 1988; Field and Jackson, 1989; Naina Patel, 1990; Farleigh, 1990; Bowling, 1990). Age Concern's ethnic minority development officer (cited Norman, 1985) who is responsible for organising services for black and ethnic minorities, undertook a review of policy among London Age Concern organisations. He commented on 'the lack of commitment and enthusiasm' generated by the subject and concluded that the typical reaction has been that older people in these communities must use the services provided.[4] Similarly, Field and Jackson (1989) concluded that Asian people were not obtaining the access to services they should because of 'ethnocentrism, discrimination and racism, and sins of omission'. Norman (1985) described 'a long established voluntary sector' that does not recognise that we live in a multi-cultural society – whether in employment policy, staff and volunteer training, committee membership, relationships with ethnic minority voluntary organisations or provision of services to individuals in minority groups. The small amount of empirical research undertaken in this area has confirmed these conclusions (Dungate, 1984; Sedley, 1989; Rooney and McKain, 1990).

---

[4] Age Concern England subsequently produced a training video, 'According to Need', for voluntary and statutory agencies. It aimed to challenge myths and assumptions and help service practitioners develop strategies to provide appropriate services, as well as encourage the development and implementation of equal opportunities policies.

The National Council of Voluntary Organisations (NCVO) conducted a postal survey of 192 NCVO members from health and social welfare organisations in 1984. Fifty-one organisations completed the question-naire, while 25 chose to reply by letter (Dungate, 1984). Several organisations who replied by letter seemed to ignore the issue either by stating the agency was 'open to all' or 'everyone is treated the same'. One letter, for instance, said:

> The sad fact is that we have practically no clients in any ethnic minority group. Our charity is open to all regardless of race, sex, colour or creed and yet out of many thousands of members we can only think of two or three people who come into the category of ethnic minorities. Frankly, we don't know why this is.

And other responses perpetuated a familiar myth:

> It happens that we have very little call for help from the ethnic minorities, athough the staff in the field represent them and I can only assume that their approach to help is somewhat different from our own. I believe that they have a pride in themselves and because they live together as families in such large numbers, they are rather more self-supporting.

Of the 51 organisations who responded to the questionnaire, only eight could provide a statistical breakdown of their clients by ethnic minority groups. Dungate suggested that most national organisations did not know, therefore, if they were reaching ethnic minority clients. Only four organisations felt they were reaching all potential clients and one did not answer the question. The remaining 46 respondents gave several reasons for their failure to reach potential ethnic minority clients. These included:

- failure to publicise services effectively
- inadequate resources (eg funding, staffing levels)
- assumptions made about ethnic minority lifestyles/culture (responses such as 'they look after their own' and 'no tradition of membership of voluntary organisations')
- language difficulties
- problems related to services offered (responses included 'white image'; 'services geared to western culture'; 'we don't do enough to seek them out'; and 'inexperience in the race field')
- cultural misunderstandings
- under-representation.

These responses, Dungate argued, raised four important issues about the relationship between the voluntary sector and black minorities.

First, while lack of resources can present problems, it can also mask the low priority accorded to working with people from ethnic minorities. Secondly, some organisations were latching onto socio-cultural explanations for certain behaviour ascribed to different ethnic groups. As a result, stereotyping and generalising at the expense of recognising individual differences were increasingly evident. Thirdly, although translating leaflets and publicity material was a useful way of reaching different groups, the written word is not necessarily the most effective form of publicity, unless there is some follow-up work. Fourthly, it may be easier to blame the potential client group for experiencing specific problems or failing to understand an organisation's aims, than it is to examine the overall relevance of the service provided.

When examining how national voluntary organisations had adapted their services to encourage ethnic minority clients, the NCVO survey found that 29 of the 51 organisations had made no changes (Dungate, 1984). Planned changes indicated by the responses included special dietary provision, changes in staff recruitment and training methods, translation of literature, and the setting up of specialist projects for ethnic minorities. In relation to equal opportunities policy the responses indicated that most organisations were unclear about what such a policy was, and many had no awareness of the detailed monitoring and follow-up procedures such policies would involve. Dungate concluded that, despite their willingness to change and adapt to a multi-racial society, national voluntary organisations did not know how to make their services more widely available and relevant.

More recent work by Sedley (1989) indicates that little change has taken place since the NVCO survey. Her review of four national voluntary organisations – The Down's Syndrome Association, National Council for One Parent Families, Maternity Alliance, and Family Service Units – suggested that none was fully prepared for the challenge of an anti-racist strategy in either employment procedures or service delivery.

The Health and Race Project survey of 70 voluntary organisations in Liverpool generated similar results (Rooney and McKain, 1990). The sample included a wide range of organisations, from self-help organisations which focused on a particular illness, through bodies like the St John Ambulance Brigade, Red Cross and various hospital Leagues of Friends, to large, relatively well-funded agencies like Barnardos and Liverpool Personal Service Society. The survey found that in an area with large black communities 98 per cent of management committees were white, 99 per cent of the users were white, 98 per cent of the employees were white, and 99 per cent of the volunteers were white. Only eight per cent of the organisations had a written policy which addressed the issue of race. The issue of racial inequality was thus not yet on the agenda of the substantial majority of organisations. The report concluded:

The organisations in the sample employ the services of people who, overwhelmingly, are white and provide their services to people who, overwhelmingly, are white. They are organised by, with and for the white community. Black people are not involved in any role, as committee members, volunteers, members or users, to any significant extent. (Rooney and McKain, 1990)

## Future policy and mainstream voluntary provision

In examining the changes taking place within mainstream voluntary services during the 1980s, Connelly (1990) described two polarised approaches to change. Some national voluntary organisations do not recognise that the multi-racial, multi-cultural, multi-lingual nature of British society has any significant implications for their roles and responsibilities. At the other extreme, some organisations are so overwhelmed by a sense of outrage and the amount of work that has to be done, that they become disabled. The position of most organisations is somewhere between such apathy and outrage. Connelly (1990) identified a need for more research, which described individual organisations' experience of change while exploring problems and solutions.

Field and Jackson (1989) argued that voluntary organisations need to take action to ensure their services are open to ethnic minority groups. While this may require special measures, it is important not to characterise services as meeting 'special' or 'additional' needs of Asian people: rather the measures should be seen as ensuring equality of provision. Finally Field and Jackson (1989) suggested the policy response of the mainstream voluntary sector should be a 'positive and overt rejection of racism'. Organisations need to take practical steps to combat racism.

Besides creating pressure for change within voluntary organisations themselves, the statutory sector has a potentially important role to play in the future policy and practice of voluntary organisations. Recent government policy envisages social services moving away from providing services to becoming purchasers and managers of care packages. Community health services will adopt a similar role. Voluntary organisations will tender for contracts to provide these services and consequently statutory provision is seen as having an obligation to ensure that voluntary provision is not racist (Shabira Moledina, 1988). Local authorities, when drawing up the contract should, first, commit the voluntary agency to racial equality and equal opportunity, and secondly, ensure that the agency provides evidence proving their competence to provide services effectively (Connelly, 1990; Rooney and McKain, 1990).

## Voluntary sector services provided by black people

The importance of black voluntary organisations in meeting the community care needs of black people is well established (Lalljie, 1983; Norman, 1985; Blakemore, 1985; Glendenning and Pearson, 1988; Farleigh, 1990; Eribo, 1991; Phaure, 1991). One of the main reasons for the growth of these organisations appears to be a lack of appropriate and adequate mainstream service provision for black communities (Bandana Ahmad, 1988b). Glendenning and Pearson (1988) for example, argue that the black and ethnic minority voluntary sector has clearly filled 'a major and appalling' gap in statutory service provision for older people in their communities.

The literature describes the growing number of community projects designed to meet the needs of, and provide support for, members of ethnic minority communities (Lalljie, 1983; Norman, 1985; Hardingham, 1988; Bowling, 1990; Pharoah and Redmond, 1991). These black voluntary organisations not only provide alternative community services to black people but also subsidise and complement statutory provision. They provide services to communities where local health and social services are unable or unwilling to do so (Reba Bhaduri, 1988; Arshi Ahmad, 1989). Lalljie (1983) suggests that:

> Black self-help organisations have, with minimal funding, if at all, provided facilities which black elders feel to be fitting, where they can feel comfortable, and where facilities have been geared to their needs. It is the existence of such facilities that have rendered black elders visible: without them, these elders would have remained scattered and invisible.

Despite its importance in providing support to black and ethnic minorities, the literature recognises the vulnerability of the black voluntary sector (Lalljie, 1983; Phaure, 1991). A conference on service response to the needs of older people from black communities, organised by Bradford Social Services Department and Bradford University, concluded that in terms of providing what people wanted and needed, voluntary agencies had a better record than statutory agencies, but were generally felt to be doing their work on a shoestring and with little support (Jolley, 1988).

## The problems faced by black voluntary organisations

The literature identifies three major problems faced by black voluntary organisations in providing community care that can, potentially, marginalise and undermine their position.

## Limited resources

First, black organisations have struggled to develop and survive on limited resources and present funding falls short of their needs (Norman, 1985; Bandana Ahmad, 1988c; Arshi Ahmad, 1989; Jarrett, 1990; Mitchell, 1990; Rooney and McKain, 1990). An open forum on care in the community, organised by The Standing Conference of Ethnic Minority Senior Citizens (SCEMSC) painted a picture of cutbacks, withdrawn grants, transport difficulties, inadequate and inaccessible premises, 'with thousands of elderly people isolated by disability, poverty and loneliness' (May, 1989a). Daniel (1988) described similar problems for some black voluntary sector day centres and contrasted these with the conditions in local authority day centres which receive mainstream funding, are largely adequately staffed and held in premises which conform to health, safety and fire regulations.

Moreover, since most black voluntary care initiatives are dependent on temporary or short-term funding from 'special' or 'soft' budgets such as inner city monies, or Section 11 funding, they are vulnerable to funding crises (Norman, 1985; Ball, 1988; Fryer, 1989).

National or local forums, which allocate resources for community services, rarely have representation from black organisations. Access to funding is related to access to the political structure, and to the knowledge and information which enables the tailoring of bids to ideas which are currently in favour. In short, funding tends to go to those who are already organised within the mainstream (Rooney and McKain, 1990).

Some writers have called for the commitment of resources to develop and sustain voluntary organisations within black communities (Daniel, 1988; Rooney and McKain, 1990; Johnson, 1991) and this is particularly important within the context of the 'contract economy'. The pressures on local authorities to achieve low unit cost will force them into block contracts with large-scale service providers (Local Government Information Unit, 1990). There is a danger that the black voluntary sector could become 'squeezed out' by large private or national voluntary care agencies (Williams, 1990; Johnson, 1991), resulting in standardised community services which are insensitive to the needs of black people.

## Relationship with statutory services

The second major problem faced by black voluntary organisations is the unequal power relationship between the statutory sector and the black voluntary sector. This provides the basis for potential exploitation and often rules out the possibility of partnership and joint work, since the statutory and mainstream agencies usually define the terms and conditions of the partnership.

Farleigh (1990) for instance, described no shortage of black organisations, even within a small black community in Brighton, but concluded that the organisations are not involved in the established voluntary sector, nor in the consultative forums with statutory services. Bishop *et al.* (1992) came to a similar conclusion. May (1989a) described a reluctance on the part of statutory and mainstream voluntary agencies to initiate any mechanism for consultation with the black voluntary sector. As a result, 'black voluntary organisations have found themselves in constrained predicaments and experienced frustration, further disappointment, reinforced mistrust and increased disparity' (Bandana Ahmad, 1988c). A seminar organised for black organisations by the National Institute of Social Work (cited Bandana Ahmad, 1988c) concluded that black communities and their organisations cannot form effective partnerships with the statutory sector unless their voices are heard and their proposals included in the restructuring of the partnership arrangements.

## Expectations

The third problem faced by black voluntary organisations in providing community care, is that statutory provision expects too much of them. Field and Jackson (1989) for instance, suggest that it is unrealistic to expect the black voluntary sector to provide services equivalent to those of the mainstream voluntary sector. Glendenning and Pearson (1988), similarly, argued that although community-based projects and self-help organisations provide support and facilities for older members of black and ethnic minority communities, few are able to reach the most frail and disabled people, or indeed to 'provide the coverage of services needed by their communities'.

There is also an inherent danger in the assumption that the existence of a black voluntary sector somehow solves 'the problem' and absolves statutory services of any responsibility for the social care needs of black minorities. The existence of a black voluntary sector, although important in responding to the needs of black communities in the absence of appropriate statutory services, does not imply that the needs of black people are being met adequately (Naina Patel, 1990; Dourado, 1991). Naina Patel (1990) further points out that most projects are small-scale, often at an 'experimental' phase, and therefore cannot be expected to serve all black older people in the country. To overcome these problems statutory services need to develop a more constructive working relationship with black voluntary groups by appreciating not only the valuable contribution made by them but also the constraints they face.

## Conclusions

Recent government policy promoting the contracting out of community services will result in the voluntary sector growing increasingly important as a provider of community services. Overwhelming evidence suggests that voluntary services are, however, not in a position to meet the social care needs of people from black and ethnic minorities.

Mainstream voluntary provision is ethnocentric, and although there is an expressed willingness to change, national voluntary organisations do not know how to make their services more widely available and relevant. Black voluntary services face the problems of operating within a racist and ethnocentric context which can marginalise and undermine their position. These include limited resources, the unequal relationship with statutory services, and high expectations held by statutory provision.

# Recommendations for future research

This review has revealed substantial gaps in knowledge about black people's experience of social care and of the services provided to support them in the community. At present, rapid developments in practice are proceeding on the basis of a poor understanding of the needs and views of older black and disabled people and those who care for them. This is perhaps ironic given the current policy emphasis on users' views and individual choice. There is therefore a clear and urgent need for research, closely linked to policy and practice, which fills these gaps. This chapter sets out an agenda for future research. The highly politicised nature of the subject, however, also demands a more theoretical insight. By exploring the policy assumptions implicit in current policy and research, the second part of the chapter will locate this agenda in a more speculative context by pointing the way to an anti-racist methodology. The intention is to stimulate a process of questioning which brings into focus a series of complex theoretical issues about the nature of policy and the production of knowledge.

## Ethnicity, disability and informal care

To understand social care needs among black minorities it is necessary to explore the character of black minorities living in the United Kingdom, the nature and experience of disability, and the circumstances and experience of informal care.

### Ethnicity
The question on ethnicity included in the 1991 census will increase the amount and sophistication of the demographic data available on black minorities. In particular, two demographic issues are relevant to developing community care policy. First, research needs to explore the composition of black minority groups in terms of age and gender, household composition, social class, unemployment, housing conditions and tenure, and education. The relationship between these variables not only affects the population of those who need care, and of those who take on the responsibility of informal care, but also the experience and circumstances of social care. Secondly, it is necessary

for research to determine the composition of black minority groups in terms of ethnic origin, and their distribution within the United Kingdom. To be responsive to local needs, policy and practice must take account of these variations.

## Disability

Future research on disability needs to address two issues. The first concerns the health status and incidence of disability among the black populations of Britain. The second is more concerned with the experience of disability among black communities and its implications for social care.

First, although the number of surveys assessing the physical health of black people is slowly growing, relatively little is known nationally about the health status or incidence of disability among Britain's ethnic minorities. The census will not provide detailed data on disability[5] and previous work by OPCS, such as the 1988 disability surveys and the 1985 and 1990 General Household Surveys, did not produce a sufficiently large sample of black and ethnic minority people. The data that exist seem contradictory. Some studies, for example, demonstrate that black people are more likely to be disabled than the white population, whereas other work suggests the incidence of disability is the same. Furthermore, material concerning the incidence of learning difficulties, mental health and dementia is non-existent. More work is clearly necessary.

Secondly, we still lack an adequate account of what health, disability and illness mean to black minorities. In this context, individual actors' perceptions and meanings become especially important. Research from this perspective allows us to see that health, illness and disability are not objective realities but intimately connected to the way people construct their social realities. This means that similar illnesses and disabilities may be perceived, accepted and coped with in different ways depending on the social and cultural context of each individual. Research exploring these issues is fundamental to informing policy debates concerned with incorporating the patient's or client's view into service provision.

## Informal care

Future research on informal care needs to address two issues. First, available information on informal care among black communities is limited to a few small scale-studies. More large-scale, nationally based studies, determining the incidence and nature of caregiving, are therefore necessary.

---

[5] The 1991 census included, for the first time, a question on long standing illness.

Secondly, future research needs to address the experience of caregiving among black communities. The relationship between the carer and the person cared for is central to the experience of informal care, yet research tell us little about the respective needs of the carers and the cared-for person, and how these might be sensibly balanced. This is particularly important because research on disability and informal care often occur independently of each other. Future research needs to balance the two accounts to ensure appropriate and effective service delivery for both the carer and the disabled person. Other areas of potential interest include the organisation of care within families, the physical and emotional cost of care giving, the financial burden of care, factors which enable carers to continue caring, or which force them to give up, and how these differ by disability group. A good deal is known about these areas in relation to white people (Parker, 1990). Little is known, however, about the extent to which black people's experiences might differ.

## The experience of community service provision

A growing amount of work explores black people's experience of community services and social security provision. The conclusions, however, are often drawn either from small-scale studies conceptualising the issue in terms of 'knowledge' and 'use' of services, or from literature which discusses and explores the policy issues rather than presenting research findings. Consequently the debate remains speculative and exploratory and a more evaluative approach is necessary for future research.

It is important to assess not only what is provided but how it is provided, particularly since the literature demonstrates the inability of community services and social security to provide appropriate, accessible and acceptable services to black communities. Barriers to access and service use, as well as the impact of provision, become important issues for future research.

## Service delivery: policy and practice

There has, as yet, been no detailed exploration of the policy and practice of service delivery in relation to black people. The inability of service provision to consider the implications of race in the delivery and organisation of service provision makes this a particularly significant subject for future research.

### Health and social services

Few health authorities and social service departments have made any systematic attempt to consider the implications of race in the delivery and organisation of service provision. The problems faced by social and health services, although similar, occur within different organisational frameworks. This is the context in which research must be planned. Beyond this three areas seem relevant to a future programme.

The first concerns the policy context. Evaluating health and social services' operation of, and commitment to, equal opportunities policy, in both service delivery and employment, is essential. Specific areas of relevance include the employment and experience of black workers and the implementation and value of ethnic monitoring.

To provide appropriate and accessible services to people from black and ethnic minorities requires more, however, than employing staff from black and ethnic minorities and ethnic monitoring. These themes, although legitimate reactions, offer only a partial response. The second area of future work, therefore, concerns the operation, in its various guises, of institutional and individual racism.

Thirdly, many local authorities are becoming aware of the significance of race and ethnicity in formulating policy. Evidence, however, suggests that racism persists in health and social services despite a commitment to race equality. Research examining the process of change in this area, and identifying problems and solutions, would enable a more systematic approach to be adopted in the future.

## Voluntary provision

Current government policy which promotes the contracting out of community services will result in the voluntary sector growing increasingly important as the provider of community services. Consequently, evaluating voluntary sector provision will be an important part of any future programme of research. This research needs to reflect both mainstream voluntary services and those voluntary services provided by minorities for minorities.

Traditional voluntary agencies neglect the support of black communities as does statutory provision. Consequently equal opportunity policies, individual and institutional racism, and future policy and practice are all areas of relevance. Important areas for research include black users' experience of provision, and exploration of how mainstream voluntary provision can make its services more widely available and relevant.

Voluntary sector services provided by black people, for black people, raise a different set of research issues. The literature establishes the importance of black voluntary organisations in meeting the community care needs of black people. Little is known, however, about how these organisations operate. Resource issues, their role in community care, the character and effectiveness of the service provided, and their relationship with statutory service provision are clearly important future research concerns. Monitoring the effect of new contracting arrangements on black voluntary organisations will be essential.

## Race research and policy: an anti-racist methodology

The first part of this chapter established an agenda for practice-related and empirical research on black people's experience of social care and the services provided to them in the community. Undertaking research among black communities, however, invites controversy and the literature documents many practical and theoretical problems (Rex, 1973; Iganski, 1990; Atkin, 1991a and 1991b). Developing and implementing social policy on race issues raise similar difficulties (Denney, 1985: Williams, 1989). Racism is central to the problems faced by research and social policy, making it necessary to challenge implicit assumptions in current provision and research (Lawrence, 1982). Tacit racist assumptions can be disguised within supposedly dispassionate and objective accounts. Consequently a 'value free' position can be seen as spurious, with an anti-racist methodology being central to a successful research and policy strategy. The second part of the chapter will thus locate this review in a more theoretical context and question the assumptions implicit in policy and practice.

### Weaknesses of existing research and policy approaches

*Cultural pluralism and ethnic diversity*
Much of the policy debate on race, in explaining differences between the majority white population and minority black population, conceptualises the issue in terms of cultural pluralism and ethnic diversity (Pearson, 1983a). In this view, diversity in language, religion, cultural norms and expectations prevents effective communication and creates misunderstanding between the majority and distinct minorities. 'Problems', the argument goes, result because of a mismatch between minority and majority cultures (Lawrence, 1982). Achieving harmony therefore requires promoting understanding of each other's culture.

Instead of creating better understanding, however, this approach misrepresents the situation. The relationship between ethnically distinct minorities and the majority white society is seen exclusively in terms of cultural practices and language differences. Within this largely uncritical framework attention is focused on the minority culture, thus diverting attention from the wider power relationships within society. This approach also fails to recognise that the dominant white culture and the distinct minority culture do not meet on equal terms.

The situation of black people cannot be understood within a political vacuum. The political, social and economic positions of black people are integral intervening factors. The circumstances of older people in Britain illustrate this point well. Most older people, black and white, encounter oppressive social conditions. The patterns of disadvantage they face, such as bad housing and environment, poverty and low income, as well as social isolation, low social status and relative lack of power, have been well documented (Norman, 1980; Phillipson, 1982; Walker, 1987; Fennell *et al.*, 1989). Black older people, however, are usually further disadvantaged. As a result of underemployment or recent arrival they seldom have occupational pensions and are often ineligible for full state pensions. Their incomes are, therefore, likely to be lower than those of white older people (Norman, 1985). Evidence also suggests that black older people experience lower social status than white older people (Norman, 1985).

Further, an exclusive pre-occupation with the cultural practices of black people results in an implicit racism within policy discussion. Black culture becomes classified according to the white norm. One of the consequences of this is the creation of a black pathology. Much of the research on black minority groups, for example, concentrates on cultural habits which become identified as a 'problem'. Black culture becomes identified in terms of an 'abnormality' which has to be regulated and rehabilitated. The assumed 'solution' is to change black people's lives, rather than begin to understand and accept them. Black communities thus tend to experience the controlling aspects of welfare provision, rather than the caring aspects (Ratna Dutt, 1989a). Examples described below, drawn from the field of health, illustrate this.

White policy 'experts' often note that black people's morbidity and response to health and illness are different from those of the dominant white group. This difference then becomes equated with deviance. The 1965 White Paper on Commonwealth Immigration provided the first tangible government response to the health issues posed by black and ethnic minority communities (Home Office, 1965). Policy had at this stage already begun to classify black people as a pathological and deviant group and argued that many 'immigrants' would for a variety of reasons continue to impose a relatively heavy burden on the health services. Between 1956 and 1971, for example, the British Medical Association passed 21 resolutions urging some form of medical examination of new immigrants (Brent Community Health Council, 1981).

Following this, Kiple and King (1981) suggest that in health matters black people suffer twice: once from the disease itself and secondly because their health problems are turned against them. Black 'health problems' are often identified as arising from cultural practice and the cause becomes located in the minorities themselves. Goel *et al.* (1981) for example, stated that the long-term answer to 'Asian rickets' lay in a change towards a western diet and lifestyle. Rocheron (1988) suggested the Asian Mother and Baby Campaign raised similar issues. The problems which the campaign associated with Asian women's care were restricted either to private or the biological/medical matters. In either case, cultural aspects were highlighted, with no reference to race or class and consequently, Rocheron concluded, the campaign colluded with an image of 'black pathology'.

Similarly, the higher disability rate among Asian communities is attributed to diet, first cousin marriages, and Asian medicines (Pearson, 1983b). This serves to reinforce the belief that Asian cultural practices are harmful to health, requiring modification. There is, in fact, no evidence to support any of these assertions and because of the preoccupation with cultural practices, other explanations – such as the role of poverty in causing ill-health – are rarely mentioned.

## Myths, stereotypes and generalisations

Besides the mistaken emphasis on cultural practices in explaining the situation of black minorities, another consequence of multi-cultural approaches is the inadequate conceptualisation of these cultural practices, grounded in vast generalizations. This further serves to undermine the position of black people. By providing over-generalised mechanical summaries of key cultural characteristics, there is a dual danger both of assuming that this knowledge somehow solves the 'problem' and of perpetuating and reinforcing cultural stereotypes and myths. Introductory notes on black communities, present in most training material for service practitioners, for example, often follow this pattern. An extract from a handbook written for community nurses illustrates this:

> Health professionals dislike being authoritarian and aim to achieve change by reasoned persuasion, but our experience is that Asian women prefer a blunter approach and are not offended by imperatives. (Karseras and Hopkins, 1987).

Over-generalised cultural summaries are insufficient in explaining the lives of black people. First, they imply that black culture is unitary and monolithic. Black minorities in Britain are not an homogeneous group. Although one would expect broad commonalities among black groups in terms of their experience of migration, general racism and so on, one would also expect differences. Secondly, generalised cultural summaries represent thoughts, feelings and action as static or inflexible. Life, however, is dynamic and contradictory. The experience of black people living in Britain illustrates this. Black people need to reconcile two or more cultural backgrounds. Cultural ties with their place of origin may still be strong yet they become faced with situations where they have to accommodate western ways and values. They have anchorage in two or more distinct cultures but do not fully belong to either (Park, 1950).

Apala Chowdhury (1989), for example, argues that Asian peoples parade an identity that becomes cultivated, carved and distorted by a culture that is both Asian and British. She argues that this creates something that is 'beautifully complete', but also 'open and uneven' where the elements of the two different cultures have failed to blend. For black peoples living in Britain it is not a matter of forsaking one culture for another but of creating the space to express both.

### Black people and special need

Policy debates often classify black people as having special needs. People from black minorities, although sometimes having different needs from the majority white population, do not necessarily have special needs. To consider that they do implies that black minorities are deviant, with their 'distinctiveness' identified as a problem. Until recently, for example, the *Social Service Abstracts* printed by the Department of Health and Social Security Libraries, included literature on ethnic minorities under the 'special needs' heading. Since this section also included poverty, homelessness, violence, probation and alcohol and drug dependency, this implied that people from black minorities formed a pathological group.

Such forms of classification segregate black people from the general debate about social care, isolating them from the mainstream discussion. Yet questions concerning the range, quality and accessibility of community service provision are applicable to all. This is not to argue that the needs of black people are the same as those of white people – the discussion must also recognise their distinctiveness – but that race must become a fundamental, but not separate, part of this debate.

## Community care and race: an agenda for action

This review outlines an agenda for practice-related research as well as establishing the general unsuitability of existing service provision to black communities. Community provision has not generally been responsive to the views of black users and this assumes importance for those planning and implementing support and care within a multi-racial society. Successful community care, in a multi-racial society, cannot therefore rely merely on an understanding of black users' views. As the review illustrates, perceptions of black people do not occur in a void but are interpreted, framed and acted upon by service providers, using judgements which may be inherently racist. This, in effect, provides the context in which black user views will be incorporated.

Consequently, besides eliciting users' views, future policy and research must also appraise the organisation and delivery of services to black people, since these provide the context in which ideas about race are transformed into practice. To carry this appraisal forward successfully more information as well as a commitment to change is necessary. At present developments are proceeding on a crude and poor understanding of the relationship between black people and service delivery. This undermines the objective of efficient, effective and equitable provision for all.

Leaving aside the need for fundamental change in provision to black people, much remains to be known about the nature and extent of community care in black communities, and about the delivery of services to black people. The research agenda outlined above reflects this. Besides discussing specific details, however, it is important to challenge the assumptions implicit in much policy and practice. Three general points have particular relevance.

- We need to avoid the danger that race issues become insulated and isolated from general discussion of social care issues, thereby marginalising the needs of black people. The issues of the range, quality and accessibility of service provision, although having to reflect different needs, are relevant to all. Rather than being regarded as a 'special needs' group, race must become an integrated part of the future debate on social care.

- Any future research and policy programme must have a strong commitment to an anti-racist methodology. When writing about the situation of black people it is important to avoid racist judgements, which undermine the legitimacy of black people's views. An account of community care in terms of black people's perceptions, without these perceptions becoming identified as deviant or pathological, must inform research and policy. A fundamental aspect of this is a recognition of the political, social and economic disadvantages faced by black people. Institutional racism is central to this disadvantage.

- Researchers also need to reflect on their role in a field where the recipients of research findings have expressed considerable scepticism about the usefulness of these findings, suggesting that research has often been a substitute for action, and a way of diverting attention from black people's problems. Future research, therefore, needs to be closely connected to practice and seen as a means of achieving change.

Community care is at a crossroads. Much radical change is in process, with important implications for black people, particularly the extent to which their needs are recognised in the change. Certainly recent policy debates have begun to assimilate some notion of a multi-racial Britain. This assimilation takes place within a wider policy context that emphasises user views, consumerism and individual choice. Service users should have an increasing say in community services, with service provision individually-led rather than service-based. Successful community service provision thus allows for a range of options for the individual user, and thereby becomes tailored to individual need. For black minorities, the way of achieving this is to understand, and to incorporate into service provision, the black user's view. Indeed evidence suggests that community service provision would benefit from closer links with the everyday experience of black people (Glendenning and Pearson, 1988; Atkin *et al.*, 1989a; Ballard, 1989; Connelly, 1989).

The problem, however, is how to forge closer links within the present ethnocentric and racist context of service delivery. To incorporate the views of black users, the debate needs to alter its present assumptions. The 'distinctiveness' of people needs to be viewed from a perspective which rejects notions of 'inferiority' and 'deviance'. Difference is not a problem in itself and the notion of 'otherness' does not address the extent to which the 'taken-for-granted' norms of the white majority are equally socially constructed. As Ballard (1989) argues, it is not that black minorities are culturally different, rather we are all different culturally.

# Key studies cited in the review

## Introduction

The review draws on various empirical studies and these are identified in this appendix. It is in two parts. The first part outlines studies exploring the experience of black people and the second outlines studies examining the organisation and delivery of service provision. The information given includes year and location of study, sample size and sample group.

## Studies of the experience of black people

### Community care and black minorities: general studies

| Author | Year | Location | Sample size | Sample group | Age |
|---|---|---|---|---|---|
| Anwal Bhalla and Blakemore, K. | 1981 | Birmingham | 400 | 179 Afro/ Caribbean 169 Asian 52 European | 55 and over |
| Berry, S. *et al.* | 1981 | Nottingham | 148 | Afro/ Caribbean | 55 and over |
| Barker, J. | 1984 | Manchester London | 619 | 234 Afro/ Caribbean 370 Asian 15 African | 55 and over |
| Donaldson, L.J. and Odell, A. | 1986 | Leicester | 726 | Asian | 65 and over |
| Donovan, J. | 1986 | London | 30 | 16 Afro/ Caribbean 14 Asian | All ages |
| Farrah, M. | 1986 | Leicester | 109 | 109 Afro/ Caribbean | 55 and over |
| Johnson, M. | 1986 | West Midlands | 1147 | 365 Afro/ Caribbean 867 Asian 915 White | 60 and under |

| Author | Year | Location | Sample size | Sample group | Age |
|---|---|---|---|---|---|
| Holland, B. and Lewando-Hundt, G. | 1987 | Coventry | 1234 260 | 71 Afro/ Caribbean 1163 Asian | 55 and over |
| British Gas Report on Attitudes to Ageing | 1991 | National | 122 128 | Afro/ Caribbean Asian | 55 and over |
| Tameside Black Elderly Working Group | 1987 | Tameside | 186 | Asian | 50 and over |
| Fenton, S. | 1987 | Bristol | 203 | 101 Afro/ Caribbean 102 Asian | 55 and over |
| Shabira Moledina | 1988 | Brent | 23 | Asian | Elderly |
| McFarland, E. et al. | 1989 | Glasgow | 60 | Asian | All ages |
| Atkin, K. et al. | 1989 | Birmingham | 162 | 84 Asian 12 Afro/ Caribbean 66 White | 55 and over 65 and over 65 and over |
| Field, S. and Jackson, H. | 1989 | London | 1000 | 517 Asian 497 White | All ages |

# Community care and black minorities: studies of informal care

| Author | Year | Location | Sample size | Sample group | Age |
|---|---|---|---|---|---|
| Lee, M. | 1987 | Nottingham | 26 | 8 Afro/Caribbean 18 Asian | Parents of children and adults with learning difficulties |
| Walker, C. | 1987 | Leeds | 16 | Asian | Parents of children with learning difficulties |
| Saroj Bulsara | 1988 | Leicester | 40 | Asian | General |
| Baxter, C. | 1989 | Manchester | 9 | 3 Asian 3 Afro/Caribbean 3 Chinese | Carers of people with cancer |
| Yasmin Gunaratnum | 1990 | London | 33 | Asian | General |
| Cole, J. | 1990 | Lewisham | 20 | Black | General |
| London Borough of Camden | 1990 | Camden | – | Black and ethnic minorities | Female carers |
| McCalman, J.A. | 1990 | Southwark | 34 | 13 Afro/Caribbean 8 Asian 13 Vietnamese/Chinese | General |
| Iseult Cocking and Surinder Athwal | 1990 | Coventry | 38 | 23 Asian 15 White | Carers of a family member with a learning difficulty |
| Jowell, T. Larrier, C. Lawrence, R. | 1990 | Birmingham | 48 | 24 Afro/Caribbean 24 Asian | General |
| Eribo, L. | 1991 | London | 51 | Afro/Caribbean | General |
| Wallace, L. | 1991 | Birmingham | 50 | Black | Carers of older people |

## Studies of service provision

### Studies of community service provision

| Author | Year | Location | Sample group |
|---|---|---|---|
| Evers *et al.* | 1989 | Birmingham | Social workers, home help organisers, occupational therapists, community nurses and community psychiatric nurses |
| Baxter *et al.* | 1990 | National | Health education authorities, social service departments and community health councils |

### Studies of social service provision

| Author | Year | Location | Sample group |
|---|---|---|---|
| Hughes, R. and Reba Bhaduri | 1986/87 | North West | Senior social service managers and social workers |
| Dearnley, J. and Milner, I.W. | 1986 | South Yorkshire | 3 social service departments |
| Prime, R. | 1987 | London | 3 social service departments |
| Cypher, J. | 1988 | West Midlands | 3 social service departments |
| Townsend, D. and Etherington, S. | 1988 | National | 43 social service departments |
| The Commission for Racial Equality | 1989 | National | 70 social service departments |
| Jabeer Butt | 1991 | National | Social service departments |

### Studies of health service provision

| Author | Year | Location | Sample group |
|---|---|---|---|
| Wright, C. | 1983 | Newcastle | 39 GPs |
| Foster, M.C. | 1988 | South East | 48 Health visitors |

## Studies of voluntary service provision

| Author | Year | Location | Sample group |
|---|---|---|---|
| Dungate, M. | 1984 | National | National Council Voluntary Organisation members |
| Rooney, B. and McKain, J. | 1990 | Liverpool | 70 voluntary health organisations |
| Phaure, S. | 1991 | Ealing, Brent, Wandsworth | 9 local voluntary organisations |

## Studies of social security provision

| Author | Year | Location | Sample group |
|---|---|---|---|
| NACAB | 1991 | National | 91 CABX and 252 case examples |

# Bibliography

ACKLAND, T. and SIRIWARDENA, S. (1989) 'Integration and segregation in an Asian community', *New Community*, 15, 4, 565–76.

ADVANCE (1988) *Black People and Volunteering: A Report on a Survey*, London: Advance.

AGAR, M. (1990) 'Invisible and in the dark', *Community Care*, 821, 28–9.

ARSHI AHMAD (1989) 'Contracting out of equal opportunities', *Social Work Today*, 21, 8, 26.

ARSHI AHMAD (1990) *Practice With Care*, London: Race Equality Unit.

BANDANA AHMAD (1988a) 'The development of social work practice and policies on race', *Social Work Today*, 19, 19, 9.

BANDANA AHMAD (1988b) 'Community social work: sharing the experience of ethnic groups', *Social Work Today*, 19, 45, 13.

BANDANA AHMAD (1988c) 'When sharing assumptions can pave the way to partnership', *Social Work Today*, 20, 15, 12.

BANDANA AHMAD (1988d) 'Turning the key to employment', *Social Work Today*, 20, 7, 27.

BANDANA AHMAD (1989a) 'Redressing imbalances with ethnic monitoring', *Social Work Today*, 20, 48, 27.

BANDANA AHMAD (1989b) 'Black pain, white hurt', *Social Work Today*, 21, 16, 29.

AHMAD, W.I.U. (1989) 'Policies, pills and political will: a critique of policies to improve the health status of ethnic minorities', *The Lancet*, 8630, 1, 148–50.

AHMAD, W.I.U. (1992) *The Politics of 'Race' and Health*, Race Relations Unit, University of Bradford and Bradford and Ilkley Community College.

AHMAD, W.I.U., KERNOHAN, E.E.M. and BAKER, M.R. (1989) 'Health of British Asians: a research review', *Community Medicine*, 11, 49–56.

ANDERSON, J.M. (1986) 'Ethnicity and illness experience: ideological structures and health care delivery systems', *Social Science and Medicine*, 22, 11, 1277–83.

ANON (1989a) 'Black staff on low grades, monitoring reveals', *Health Service Journal*, 99, 5153, 656.

ANON (1989b) 'Ethnic Minorities', *Health Services Management Journal*, 85, 3–4.

ANON (1991) 'Getting the race perspective into community care', *Caring for People*, 3, 8.

ARTLEY, A. (1987) 'Out of sight out of mind', *The Spectator*, 258, 8285, 8–10.

ASIAN CARERS PROJECT (1989) *Caring and Sharing*, video in Hindi/ English, Booklets in Gujarati/Punjabi/Bengali/Urdu and English, London: King's Fund and Health Education Authority.

ASSOCIATION OF DIRECTORS OF SOCIAL SERVICES/ COMMISSION FOR RACIAL EQUALITY (1978) *Multi-racial Britain: The Social Services Response*, London: Commission for Racial Equality.

ATKIN, K. (1991a) 'Health, illness, disability and black minorities: a speculative critique of present day discourse', *Disability, Handicap and Society*, 6, 1, 37–47.

ATKIN, K. (1991b) 'Community care in a multi-racial society: incorporating user views', *Policy and Politics*, 19, 3, 159–66.

ATKIN, K. and BALDWIN, S. (1988) 1985 *General Household Survey – Questions on Informal Care*, DHSS 464 9.88, Social Policy Research Unit, University of York: York.

ATKIN, K. CAMERON, E., BADGER, F. and EVERS, E. (1989a) 'Asian elders' knowledge and future use of community social and health services', *New Community*, 15, 2, 439–46.

ATKIN, K., CAMERON, E., BADGER, F. and EVERS, E. (1989b) 'Why don't general practitioners refer their disabled Asian patients to district nurses?', *Health Trends*, 1, 21, 31–2.

AUDIT COMMISSION (1986) *Making a Reality of Community Care*, London: HMSO.

BADGER, F., CAMERON, E. and GRIFFITHS, R. (1988) 'Put race on the agenda', *The Health Service Journal*, 98, 5129, 1426–27.

BADGER, F., CAMERON, E. and EVERS, H. (1990) 'Slipping through the net', *The Health Service Journal*, 100, 5184, 86–7.

BALARAJAN, R., YUEN, P. and SONI RALEIGH, V. (1989) 'Ethnic differences in general practitioner consultations', *British Medical Journal*, 299, 958–60.

BALL, H. (1988) 'The limits of influence: ethnic minorities and the partnership programme', *New Community*, 15, 1, 7–22.

BALLARD, R. (1989) 'Social Work with Black People: What's the Difference' in ROJECK, C., PEACOCK, G. and COLLINS, S. (eds) *The Haunt of Misery: Critical Essays in Social Work and Helping*, London: Routledge.

BARCLAY, P.M. (1982) *Social Workers: Their Role and Tasks*, London: Bedford Square Press.

BARKER, J. (1984) *Black and Asian Old People in Britain*, Mitcham: Age Concern Research Unit.

BARTLETT, N. (1989) 'A moving target', *Community Care*, 786, 1–2.

BAXTER, C. (1987) 'Steps to sensitising the service', *The Health Service Journal*, 97, 5053, 642–3.

BAXTER, C. (1988) 'Black carers in focus', *Carelink*, 4, 4–5.

BAXTER, C. (1989a) *Cancer support and ethnic minority and migrant work communities*, London: CancerLink.

BAXTER, C. (1989b) 'Unequal partnerships', *Nursing Times*, 85, 70–1.

BAXTER, C., KAMALJIT POONIA, WARD, L. and ZENOBIA NADIRSHAW (1990) *Double Discrimination*, London: King's Fund/ Commission for Racial Equality.

BEAVER, R., HENDRY, B. and MARSTON, S. (1989) 'A more positive attitude', *Social Services Insight*, 4, 2, 19–20.

NASA BEGUM (1992) *Something to be Proud of: The Lives of Asian People and Carers in Waltham Forest*, Race Relations Unit and Disability Unit, London Borough of Waltham Forest.

BERRY, S., LEE, M. and GRIFFITHS, S. (1981) *Report on a Survey of West Indian Pensioners in Nottingham*, Nottingham Social Services Department: Nottingham.

REBA BHADURI (1988) 'Coming in from the cold', *Social Services Insight*, 3, 8, 12–14.

REBA BHADURI (1989) 'A prescription for counselling', *Social Work Today*, 21, 14, 16–17.

REBA BHADURI and WRIGHT, R. (1990) *Social Services and Members of Black and Minority Ethnic Communities: A Study of Policies and Programmes in Nine Social Service Departments*, London: Social Services Inspectorate.

ANWAL BHALLA and BLAKEMORE, K. (1981) *Elderly of the Minority Ethnic Groups*, Birmingham: All Faiths for One Race.

ASHOK BHAT, CARR-HILL, R. and SUSHUL OHRI (eds) (1988) *Britain's Black Populations*, Aldershot: Gower.

BHOPAL, R.S. and DONALDSON, L.J. (1988) 'Health education for ethnic minorities – current provision and future direction', *Health Education Journal*, 47, 4, 137–40.

BISHOP, N., AMINA, M. and WILLIAMS, B. (1992) 'Black voluntary organisations in the care market', *Share*, 4, 4–5.

BLAKEMORE, K. (1982) 'Health and illness among the elderly of minority ethnic groups living in Birmingham: some new findings', *Health Trends*, 14, 3, 69–72.

BLAKEMORE, K. (1985) 'The state, the voluntary sector and new developments in provision for old minority racial groups', *Ageing and Society*, 5, 175–99.

BOTTOMLEY, V. (1993) 'My new year resolution for the NHS', *The Health Service Journal*, 7 Jan.

BOULD, M. (1990a) 'Trapped within four walls', *Community Care*, 810, 17–19.

BOULD, M. (1990b) 'Working for black carers', *Mutual Aid and Self Help*, 15, 1–3.

BOWES, A. and SIM, D. (1991) *Demands and Constraints: Ethnic Minorities and Social Services in Scotland*, Edinburgh: SCVO.

BOWL, R. and BARNES, M. (1991) 'Race, racism and mental health social work: implications for local authority policy and training', *Research, Policy and Planning*, 8, 2, 12–18.

BOWLING, B. (1990) *Elderly People from Ethnic Minorities: A Report on Four Projects*, London: Age Concern Institute of Gerontology.

BRADFORD SOCIAL SERVICES (1989) *Survey of Carers*, Report for Social Services Committee, City of Bradford Metropolitan Council.

BRENT COMMUNITY HEALTH COUNCIL (1981) *Black People and the Health Service*, Brent: CHC.

BRENT SOCIAL SERVICES (1991) *Support for Carers: Carers' Views on Services in Brent*, London: Brent Social Services.

BROTCHIE, J. (1989) 'A bridge across cultures', *Community Care*, 786, ii–iii.

BROWN, C. (1984) *Black and White Britain: the Third PSI Survey*, London: Heinemann.

SAROJ BULSARA (1988) 'Services for all', *Carelink*, 6, 6.

BURNINGHAM, S. (1990) 'Surrogate families', *Social Work Today*, 21, 49, 16–17.

JABEER BUTT, GORBACK, P. and BANDANA AHMAD (1991) *Equally Fair*, London: Race Equality Unit.

CAMDEN, LONDON BOROUGH OF (1990) *The Needs of Women Carers whose First Language is not English*, Report of the Director of Law and Administration (Women's Unit), London Borough of Camden.

CAMERON, E., BADGER, F., EVERS, H. and ATKIN, K. (1989a) 'Black old women, disability and health carers', in JEFFREYS, M. (ed) *Growing Old in the Twentieth Century*, London: Routledge.

CAMERON, E., BADGER, F. and EVERS, H. (1989b) 'District nursing, the disabled and the elderly: who are the black patients?', *Journal of Advanced Nursing*, 14, 376–82.

DALONI CARLISLE (1990) 'Trying to open doors', *Nursing Times*, 86, 18, 42–3.

CASSIDY, M. and WORRALL, J. (1988) *Raising the Issues – A Review of Service Provision for the Ethnic Minorities*, Derbyshire Family Practitioner Committee.

BAL CHAUHAN (1989) 'Keeping in touch with the Asian community', *Community Care*, 764, vi–vii.

CHEETHAM, J. (1981) *Social Work Services for Ethnic Minorities in Britain and the USA*, London: DHSS.

CHEETHAM, J., JAMES, W., LONEY, M., MAYER, B and PRESCOTT, J. (1981) *Social and Community Work in a Multi-racial Society*, London: Harper and Row.

APALA CHOWDHURY (1989) 'Cultural Crossroads', *Marxism Today*, October 1989, 48–9.

ISEULT COCKING and SURINDER ATHWAL (1990) 'A special case for treatment', *Social Work Today*, 21, 22, 12–13.

COHEN, R., COXALL, J., CRAIG, G. and AZRA SADIQ (1992) *Hardship Britain: Being Poor in the 1990s*, London: CPAG/FSU.

COLE, J. (1990) *The Needs of Elderly Black People, Carers and Black People with Disabilities*, Lewisham Social Services, London: London Borough of Lewisham.

CONFEDERATION OF INDIAN ORGANISATIONS (1987) *Double Bind: To be Disabled and Asian*, London: Confederation of Indian Organisations.

CONFEDERATION OF INDIAN ORGANISATIONS (1988) *Asians and Disabilities*, London: Confederation of Indian Organisations.

CONNELLY, N. (1988a) *Caring in the Multi-racial Community*, London: Policy Studies Institute.

CONNELLY, N. (1988b) *Ethnic Record Keeping and Monitoring in Service Delivery*, London: Policy Studies Institute.

CONNELLY, N. (1989) *Race and Change in Social Services Departments*, London: Policy Studies Institute.

CONNELLY, N. (1990) *Between Apathy and Outrage: Voluntary Organisations in Multiracial Britain*, London: Policy Studies Institute.

CONROY, S. and SAFDER MOHAMMED (1989) 'Rooting out racism', *Health Service Journal*, 99, 5132, 19.

CONTACT A FAMILY (1989) *Reaching Black Families?* London: Contact a Family.

COOK, J. and WATT, S. (1987) 'Racism, women and poverty', in GLENDINNING, C. and MILLAR, J. (eds) *Hard Earned Lives*, London: Tavistock.

COOMBE, V. (1981) 'Britain's other elderly', in CHEETHAM, J. (ed) *Social and Community Work in a Multi-racial Society*, London: Harper Row.

COOPER, J. (1979) 'West Indian Elderly in Leicester: A Case Study', in GLENDENNING, F. (ed) *The Elders in Ethnic Minorities: A Report of a Seminar*, University of Keele, Beth Johnson Foundation Publications.

COOPER, S. (1985) *Observations in Supplementary Benefit Offices*, London: Policy Studies Institute.

COPE, R. (1989) 'The compulsory detention of Afro-Caribbeans under the Mental Health Act', *New Community*, 15, 3, 343–56.

COTMORE, R. (1988) *Case Studies in Service Development in Nottinghamshire: A Welfare Rights Initiative*, Loughborough: Loughborough University of Technology, Centre for Research in Social Policy.

CRAIG, G. (1991) 'Life on the Social', *Social Work Today*, 22, 28, 16–17.

CRE (1989a) *Racial Equality in Social Services Departments. A Survey of Equal Opportunity Policies*, London: Commission for Racial Equality.

CRE (1989b) *Response to the Government's White Paper on the Review of the National Health Service*, London: Commission for Racial Equality.

CROSS, M., JOHNSON, M.R.D. and COX, B. (1988) *Black Welfare and Local Government: Section 11 and Social Services Departments*, Policy Papers in Ethnic Relations, University of Warwick.

CURRER, C. (1986) 'Concepts of mental well- and ill-being: the case of pathan mothers in Britain', in CURRER, C. and STACEY, M. (eds) *Concepts of Health, Illness and Disease. A Comparative Perspective*, Leamington Spa: Berg.

CYPHER, J. (1988) *Developing Social Services for Ethnic Minority Groups: Overview Report of an Inspection of 3 West Midlands Social Services Department*, London: Social Services Inspectorate.

DANIEL, S. (1988) 'A code to care for the elders', *Social Work Today*, 19, 50, 9.

DARBY, S.J. (1989) 'Health needs of ethnic elderly epeople', *Health Visitor* 62, 304–5.

DEARNLEY, J. and MILNER, I.W. (1986) *Ethnic Minority Development (Kirklees MDC)*, London: Social Services Inspectorate.

DEARNLEY, J. and PRIME, R. (1989) *Inspection of Social Work with Afro/ Caribbean and Asian Families in Avon*, Bristol: Social Services Inspectorate, South Western Region, Department of Health and Social Security.

DENNEY, D. (1985) 'Race and crisis management', in MANNING, N. (ed) *Social Problems and Welfare Ideology*, Aldershot: Gower Press.

DEPARTMENT OF HEALTH (1989) *Caring for People: Community Care in the Next Decade and Beyond*, Cm. 849, London: HMSO.

DEPARTMENT OF HEALTH (1990) *NHS and Community Care Act*, London: HMSO.

DEPARTMENT OF HEALTH (1991) 'Getting the race perspective into community care', *Caring for People*, 3, 8.

DIBBLIN, J. (1990) 'Communication on call', *Social Work Today*, 21, 46, 25–5.

DOMINELLI, L. (1988) *Antiracist Social Work: A Challenge for White Practitioners and Educators*, Basingstoke: MacMillan Education.

DOMINELLI, L. (1989a) 'An uncaring profession? An examination of racism in social work', *New Community*, 15, 3, 391–403.

DOMINELLI, L. (1989b) 'White racism poor practice', *Social Work Today*, 20, 18, 12–13.

DONALDSON, L.J. and ODELL, A. (1986) 'Aspects of the health and social service needs of elderly Asians in Leicester: a community survey, *British Medical Journal*, 293, 1079–82.

DONOVAN, J. (1984) 'Ethnicity and race: a research review', *Social Science and Medicine*, 19, 7.

DONOVAN, J. (1986) *We don't buy sickness, it just comes*, Aldershot: Gower Press.

DOURADO, P. (1991) 'Getting the message across', *Community Care*, 856: 22–3.

DOYAL, L., HUNT, G. and MELLOR, J. (1980) *Migrant Workers in the National Health Service*, London: Polytechnic of North London.

DUNGATE, M. (1984) *A Multiracial Society, The Role of National Voluntary Organisations*, London: Bedford Square Press.

DURRANT, J. (1989) 'Moving forward in a multiracial society', *Community Care*, 792, iii–iv.

RATNA DUTT (1989a) 'Griffiths really is a white paper', *Social Work Today*, 21, 13, 34.

RATNA DUTT (1989b) 'The harsh reality for black care assistants', *Community Care*, 786, vi–vii.

RATNA DUTT (1989c) *Community Care Race Dimension*, London: Race Equality Unit.

RATNA DUTT and ARSHI AHMAD (1990) 'Griffiths and the black perspective', *Social Work and Social Sciences Review*, 2, 1, 37–44.

SHAH EBRAHIM (1990) 'Care before colour: a new look at ethnic minorities', *Geriatric Medicine*, 20, 9, 51–6.

EBRAHIM, S., PATEL, N., COATES, M., GREIG, C., GILLEY, J., BANGHAM, C. and STACEY, S. (1991) 'Prevalence and severity of morbidity among Asian elders: a controlled comparison', *Family Practice*, 8, 57–62.

ELLICE-WILLIAMS, R. (1988) 'Community care: the invisible vanguard', *Social Work Today*, 19, 40, 21.

ELLIS, B. (1990) 'Working for racial equality in health service employment', *King's Fund News*, 13, 3, 4.

ELY, P. and DENNEY, D. (1987) *Social Work in a Multi-Racial Society*, Aldershot: Gower Press.

ERIBO, L. (1991) *The Support You Need: Information for Carers of Afro/-Caribbean Elderly People*, London: Kings Fund Centre.

EVERS, H., BADGER, F., CAMERON, E. and ATKIN, K. (1989) *Community Care Project Working Papers*, Department of Social Medicine, University of Birmingham: Birmingham.

FARLEIGH, A. (1990) 'Invisible communities', *Community Care*, 806, 30–1.

FARRAH, M. (1986) 'Black elders in Leicester: an action research report on the needs of black elderly people of African descent from the Caribbean', *Social Services Research*, 1, 47–9.

FENNELL, G., PHILLIPSON, C. and EVERS, H. (1989) *The Sociology of Old Age*, Milton Keynes: Open University Press.

FENTON, S. (1987) *Ageing Minorities: Black People as They Grow Old in Britain*, London: Commission for Racial Equality.

FEWSTER, C. (1989) 'Trying in speak in tongues', *The Health Service Journal*, 99, 5161, 916–17.

FIELD, S. and JACKSON, H. (1989) *Race, Community Groups and Service Delivery*, London: HMSO.

FIELDING, N. (1990) 'A group with a difference', *Community Care*, 796, 14–15.

FOSTER, M.C. (1988) 'Health visitors' perspectives on working in a multi-ethnic society', *Health Visitor*, 61, 275–8.

FRANCIS, E. (1990) 'Community care projects for the black community – Afro-Caribbean Mental Health Association', *Care in the Community. Making it Happen*, London: HMSO.

FRY, P. (1989) 'Cultural and racial factors in social work with individuals and families', *Journal of Social Work Practice*, 3, 4, 78–85.

FRYER, R.G. (1989) *Conference on Services for Black Elders*, London: Social Services Inspectorate (East Midlands Region).

GABRIEL, S. (1989) 'Black to black', *Community Care*, 784, 26.

GILLAM, S.J., JARMAN, B., WHITE, P. and LAW, R. (1989) 'Ethnic differences in consultation rates in urban general practice', *British Medical Journal*, 299, 953–7.

GLAD (1987) *Disability and Ethnic Minority Communities – A Study in Three London Boroughs*, London: Greater London Association for Disabled People.

GLARE (1987) *In Critical Condition*, London: Greater London Action for Race Equality.

GLENDENNING, F. and PEARSON, M. (1988) *The Black and Ethnic Minority Elders in Britain: Health Needs and Access to Services*, Health Education Authority in Association with the Centre for Social Gerontology, University of Keele.

GOEL, K.M., SWEET, E.M., CAMPBELL, S., ATTENBURROW, A., LOGAN, R.W. and ARNEIL, G.C. (1981) 'Reduced Prevalence of Rickets in Asian Children in Glasgow', *The Lancet*, i, 405–7.

GOHIL, V. (1987) 'DHSS service delivery to ethnic minority claimants', *Leicester Rights Bulletin*, 32 7–8.

GORDON, P. (1986) 'Racism and social security', *Critical Social Policy*, 17, 23–40.

GORDON, P. and NEWHAM, A. (1985) *Passport to Benefits, Racism in Social Security*, London: Child Poverty Action Group and Runnymede Trust.

GRATTON, B. and WILSON, V. (1988) 'Family support systems and the minority elderly: a cautionary analysis', *Journal of Gerontological Social Work*, 13, 1/2, 81–93.

GREEN, H. (1988) *Informal Carers*, London: HMSO.

GRIFFITHS, R. (1988) *Community Care: an Agenda for Action*, London: HMSO.

GRIMSLEY, M. and ASHOK BHAT (1988) 'Racism and welfare – health', in ASHOK BHAT, CARR-HILL, R. and SUSHEL OHRI (eds) *Britain's Black Population, A New Perspective*, Aldershot: Gower Press.

GULLIFORD, F. (1984) *A Comparison Study of the Experiences and Service Needs of Bangladeshi and White Families with Severely Handicapped Children*, Unpublished dissertation for the Diploma of Clinical Psychology, Leicester: British Psychology Society.

YASMIN GUNARATNUM (1990) 'Asian carers', *Carelink*, 11, 6.

RAFAEL HALAHMY (1988) 'Falling between two cultures', *Social Work Today*, 19, 43, 12–13.

RAFAEL HALAHMY (1990) 'Slow road to equality', *Social Work Today*, 21, 46, 26.

AMBREEN HAMEED (1989) 'Black and blue', *New Statesman and Society*, 2, 46, 24–5.

HARDINGHAM, S. (1988) 'Striving for equal opportunity', *Social Services Insight*, 3, 32, 15–17.

HASKEY, J. (1991) 'The ethnic minority populations resident in private households – estimates by County and Metropolitan District of England and Wales', *Population Trends*, 63, 22–35.

HATCHETT, W. (1991) 'Open to all', *Community Care*, 854, 26–7.

HEPTINSTALL, D. (1989) 'Black and white choice for elderly consumers', *Social Work Today*, 20, 50, 12–13.

HICKS, C. (1988a) *Who Cares: Looking After People at Home*, London: Virago.

HICKS, C. (1988b) 'NHS Colourblindness', *The Health Service Journal*, 98, 5102, 590–1.

HOLLAND, B. and LEWANDO-HUNDT, G. (1987) *Coventry Ethnic Minorities Elderly Survey, Method and Data and Applied Action*, Coventry: City of Coventry Ethnic Development Unit.

HOLMES, K. (1990) 'Racism in the social services', *Public Service* (NALGO), November 1988, 6–7.

HOME OFFICE (1965) *White Paper on Commonwealth Immigration*, London: HMSO.

HORTON, C. and KARMI, G. (1992) *Guidelines for the Implementation of Ethnic Monitoring in Health Service Provision*, London: North West Thames Regional Health Authority.

GURO HUBY and SALKIND, M.R. (1990) 'Social work in the multi-cultural environment', *Journal of Social Work Practice*, 4, 2, 90–7.

HUGHES, R. (1986) *Social Services for Ethnic Minorities – Policy and Practice in the North West*, Manchester: Social Services Inspectorate, DHSS.

HUGHES, R. and REBA BHADURI (1987) *Race and Culture in Social Services Delivery: A Study in three Social Services Departments of North West England*, Manchester: Social Services Inspectorate.

HUGHES, R. and REBA BHADURI (1990) 'A model for change', *Social Services Insight*, 5, 2, 17–18.

IGANSKI, P. (1990) *Challenging Racism: Defining the Role of the White Researcher*, paper presented to the British Sociological Association Conference, University of Surrey, Guildford.

INEICHEN, B. (1987) 'The mental health of Asians in Britain a research note', *New Community*, 14, 136–41.

INEICHEN, B. (1989) 'Afro-Caribbeans and the incidence of schizo-phrenia: a review', *New Community*, 15, 3, 335–42.

JACKSON, C. (1990) 'Controversy surrounds new language line', *Health Visitor*, 63, 9, 294.

JARMAN, B. (1983) 'The identification of underprivileged areas', *British Medical Journal*, 286, 1705–9.

JARRETT, M. (1990) 'The black voluntary sector', *NCVO News*, 19, 7–8.

JENKINSON, P. (1988) 'Owning up to racism in a multi-cultural society', *Social Work Today*, 20, 5, 20–21.

JERVIS, M. (1990) 'More than just a hearing aid', *Social Work Today*, 22, 7, 19, 21.

JOHNSON, L. (1991) 'The impact of contracting on the black voluntary sector', *NCVO Newsletter*, 18, 14.

JOHNSON, M. (1986) 'Inner city residents, ethnic minorities and primary health care in the West Midlands', in RATHWELL, T. and PHILLIPS, D. (eds) *Health Race and Ethnicity*, Bexley: Croom Helm.

JOHNSON, M. (1987) 'Towards racial equality in health and welfare: what progress?', *New Community*, 14, 2, 128–35.

JOHNSON, M. (1991) 'Health and social services report', *New Community*, 17, 2, 268–9.

JOHNSON, M., COX, B. and CROSS, M. (1989) 'Paying for change?', *New Community*, 15, 3, 371–90.

JOLLEY, M. (1988) 'Ethnic minority elders want more sensitive services', *Social Work Today*, 8, 19, 19.

JONES, D. (1990) 'Working with black communities', *Carelink*, 12, 6.

JOWELL, T., LARRIER, C. and LAWRENCE, R. (1990) *Joint CCSAP/ Kings Fund Centre Action Project into the Needs of Carers in Black and Minority Ethnic Communities in Birmingham*, Birmingham: Birmingham City Council, Social Services Department.

NIRVEEN KALSI and CONSTANTINIDES, P. (1989) *Working Towards Racial Equality in Health Care, the Haringey Experience*, London: King's Fund Centre.

KARSERAS, P. and HOPKINS, E. (1987) *British Asians: Health in the Community*, Chichester: John Wily and Sons.

KEEBLE, U. (1984) *Disability and Ethnic Minority Groups. A Fact Sheet of Issues and Initiatives*, London: RADAR.

KELLY, C. (1987) 'Finding a voice', *Community Care*, 692, 22–3.

KIPLE, K.F. and KING, V.I.H. (1981) *Another Dimension to the Black Diaspora*, Cambridge: Cambridge University Press.

KNOWLES, C. (1991) 'Afro/Caribbeans and schizophrenia: how does psychiatry deal with issues of race, culture and ethnicity', *Journal of Social Policy*, 20, 2: 173–90.

LAKHANI, B. (1990a) 'Race and benefits', (Part I) *Health Visitor*, 63, 10, 356.

LAKHANI, B. (1990b) 'Race and benefits', (Part II) *Health Visitor*, 63, 11, 393.

LALLJIE, R. (1983) *Black Elders: A Discussion Paper*, Nottinghamshire County Council, Social Services Department Research Unit.

LAWRENCE, E. (1982) 'In the abundance of water the fool is thirsty: sociology and black pathology', *The Empire Strikes Back: Race and Racism in 70s Britain*, Centre for Contemporary Cultural Studies, London: Hutchinson.

LEE, M. (1987) *Sample Study of Black Families with a Mentally Handicapped Member*, Nottinghamshire County Council Social Services Department Research Unit, Nottingham.

LEVI-STRAUSS, C. (1970) *The Raw and the Cooked*, New York: Harper and Row.

LOCAL GOVERNMENT INFORMATION UNIT (1990) 'The black community and community care', *Equalities News*, 10, 1–2.

LUNN, T. (1989) 'Continuous agitation', *Community Care*, 771, 23–5.

LUNN, T. (1990) 'Consult and deliver', *Community Care*, 802, iii–iv.

MCAVOY, B.R. (1990) 'Women's Health', in MCAVOY, B.R. and DONALDSON, L.J. (eds) *Health Care for Asians*, Oxford: Oxford University Press.

MCAVOY, B.R. and DONALDSON, L.J. (eds) (1990) *Health Care for Asians*, Oxford: Oxford University Press.

MCAVOY, P. (1988) 'Find the hidden carer: a GP view', *Carelink*, 5, 2.

MCCALMAN, J.A. (1990) *The Forgotten People*, London: King's Fund Centre.

MCCRUDDEN, C., SMITH, D. and BROWN, C. (1991) *Racial Justice at Work: Enforcement of the Race Relations Act 1976 in Employment*, London: Policy Studies Institute.

MCDONALD, P. (1991) 'Double discrimination must be faced now', *Disability Now*, March, 8.

MCFARLAND, E., DALTON, M. and WALSH, D. (1989) 'Ethnic minority needs and service delivery: the barriers to access in a Glasgow inner-city area', *New Community*, 15, 3, 405–15.

MCHANWELL, J. (1989) 'A dialogue for service delivery', *Social Work Today*, 20, 45, 23.

MCNAUGHT, A. (1988) *Race and Health Policy*, Bexley: Croom Helm.

MCNAUGHT, A. (1990) 'Organisation and delivery of care', in MCAVOY, B.R. and DONALDSON, L.J. (eds) *Health Care for Asians*, Oxford: Oxford University Press.

MALLINSON, I. and BEST, E. (1990) 'Promoting power', *Social Work Today*, 21, 29, 24–5.

MARES, P., HENLEY, A. and BAXTER, C. (1985) *Health Care in Multi-Racial Britain*, Cambridge: Health Education Council and National Extension College.

MARTIN, J., MELTZER, H. and ELLIOT, D. (1988) *OPCS Survey of Disability in Great Britain: The Prevalence of Disability Among Adults*, London: HMSO.

MAY, A. (1989a) 'The minority voice in search of an audience', *The Health Service Journal*, 99, 5148, 507.

MAY, A. (1989b) 'Race: time for positive action', *The Health Service Journal*, 99, 5142, 323.

MERCER, K. (1984) 'Black communities' experience of psychiatric services', *International Journal of Social Psychiatry*, 30, 1–2, 22–7.

MIGNOTT, J. (1988) 'Rout racism by deed as well as word', *Social Work Today*, 19, 29, 28.

MILLAR, B. (1990) 'Racist, insensitive and short of money', *The Health Service Journal*, 100, 5186, 156.

MITCHELL, D. (1990) 'Contracts for equality', *Social Services Insight*, 5, 21, 15.

SAFDER MOHAMMED (1987) *No Alibi, No Excuse: A Progress Report on the Development of Equal Opportunities in London's Health Authorities*, London: Greater London Action for Race Equality.

SHABIRA MOLEDINA (1987) 'Caring for Asian elders', *Carelink*, 1, 3.

SHABIRA MOLEDINA (1988) *Great Expectations: A Review of Services for Asian Elders in Brent*, London: Age Concern Brent.

NACAB (1991) *Barriers to Benefit, Black Claimants and Social Security*, London: National Association of Citizens Advice Bureaux.

NAHA (1988) *Action not Words: A Strategy to Improve Health Services for Black and Minority Ethnic Groups*, London: National Association of Health Authorities.

NATHWANI, A. (1987) *Disability in the Asian Communities*, London: GLAD.

NATIONAL COUNCIL OF VOLUNATARY ORGANISATIONS (1991) *Section 11 – Funding for Black and Elderly Minorities? Guidance Notes for Voluntary Groups*, London: NVCO.

NEATE, P. (1989) 'The cost of carrying equal opportunities', *Community Care*, 786, vii–viii.

NORMAN, A. (1980) *Rights and Risks*, London: National Corporation for the Care of Old People.

NORMAN, A. (1985) *Triple Jeopardy: Growing Old in a Second Homeland*, Policy Studies in Ageing No 3, London: Centre for Policy on Ageing.

ABIOLA OGUNSOLA (1992) *Equality and Access: Black and Minority Ethnic People's Health Project*, Health Project for Black and Minority Ethnic Groups.

OLDMAN, C. (1990) *Moving in Old Age: New Directions in Housing Policies*, London: HMSO.

OLIVER, M. (1991) *The Politics of Disablement*, London: Macmillan.

OPCS (1983) *Census 1981: Country of Birth, Great Britain*, London: HMSO.

OPCS (1988) *The Prevalence of Disability Among Adults. OPCS Survey of Disability in Great Britain*, London: HMSO.

OPPENHEIM, C. (1990) *Poverty: The Facts*, London: CPAG.

OWUSU-BEMPAH, J. (1989a) 'Does colour matter?', *Community Care*, 747, 18–19.

OWUSU-BEMPAH, J. (1989b) 'The new institutional racism', *Community Care*, 780, 23–5.

OWUSU-BEMPAH, J. (1990) 'Toeing the white line', *Community Care*, 838: 16–17.

PAI SHAILA and KAPUR, R.L. (1981) 'The burden on the family of a psychiatric patient: development of an interview schedule', *British Journal of Psychiatry*, 138, 332–35.

PARK, R.E. (1950) *Race and Culture*, New York: The Free Press.

PARKER, G. (1990) *With Due Care and Attention: A Review of Research on Informal Care (Second Edition)*, Family Policy Studies Centre Occasional Paper No 2, London: Family Policy Studies Centre.

PATEL, NAINA (1990) *A Race Against Time, Social Services Provision to Black Elders*, London: Runnymede Trust.

PATEL, MEENA (1991) 'Reaching black carers', *Carelink*, 13, 2.

PEARSON, M. (1983a) 'Racism and myth surrounding Asian handicap', *Radical Community Medicine*, 14, 22–6.

PEARSON, M. (1983b) 'The politics of ethnic minority health studies', *Radical Community Medicine*, 16, 34–44.

PEARSON, M. (1986) 'The politics of ethnic minority health studies', in RATHWELL, T. and PHILLIPS, D. (eds) *Health, Race and Ethnicity*, Bexley: Croom Helm.

PEARSON, R.M. (1988) *Social Services in Multi-racial Society*, Social Services Inspectorate: Department of Health.

PEARSON, R.M. (1989) 'Room at the top', *Social Services Insight*, 4, 7, 12–14.

PEGRAM, A. (1988) 'Extending awareness', *Nursing Times*, 84, 35–6.

PHAROAH, C. and REDMOND, E. (1991) 'Care for ethnic elders', *The Health Service Journal*, 20–2.

PHAURE, S. (1991) *Who Really Cares? Models of Voluntary Sector Community Care and Black Communities*, London: London Voluntary Service Council.

PHILLIPS, D. (1987) 'Searching for a decent home: ethnic minority progress in the post-war housing market', *New Community*, 14, 1/2, 105–17.

PHILLIPSON, C. (1982) *Capitalism and the Construction of Old Age*, London: Macmillan.

KAMALJIT POONIA and WARD, L. (1990) 'Fair share of (the) care?', *Community Care*, 796, 16–18.

POWELL, M. and PERKINS, E. (1984) 'Asian families with a pre-school handicapped child – a study', *Mental Handicap*, 12, 50–2.

PRASHER, U. and NICOLAS, S. (1986) *Routes or Roadblocks? Consulting Minority Communities in London Boroughs*, London: Runnymede Trust.

PRIME, R. (1987) *Developing Social Services to Black and Ethnic Minority Elders in London: Overview Report and Action Plan*, London: Social Services Inspectorate.

RADAR (1984) *Disability and Minority Ethnic Groups: A Factsheet of Issues and Initiatives*, London: The Royal Association for Disability and Rehabilitation.

VEENA SONI RALEIGH (1992) 'Ethnic monitoring – the need for consistent classification', *Share*, 3, 7–8.

RANGER, C. (1989) 'Strategy needed for services to ethnic groups', *Social Work Today*, 21, 6, 16–17.

RATHWELL, T. (1984) 'General practice, ethnicity and health services delivery', *Social Science and Medicine*, 19, 2, 123–30.

RATHWELL, T. and PHILLIPS, D. (eds) (1986) *Health, Race and Ethnicity*, Bexley: Croom Helm.

REDDING, D. (1990) 'Suffering in silence', *Community Care*, 842, 17–19.

RENSHAW, J. (1989) 'Priority for health', *The Health Service Journal*, 99, 5154, 701.

REX, J. (1973) *Race Relations in Sociological Theory*, London: Routledge and Kegan Paul.

RHODES, P. (1991) 'The assessment of black fosterparents: the relevant of cultural skills – comparative views of social workers and applicants', *Critical Social Policy*, 32, 31–51.

RICHARDSON, A., UNELL, J. and ASTIN, B.A. (1989) *A New Deal for Carers*, London: Kings Fund.

ROACH, D. (1989) 'Employment and recruitment of black staff', *Community Care*, 761, i–ii.

ROBINSON, J. and STALKER, C. (1992) *New Directions – Suggestions for Improving Take-up in Short-term Breaks*, London: HMSO.

ROCHERON, Y. (1988) 'The Asian mother and baby campaign: the construction of ethnic minorities' health needs', *Critical Social Policy*, 22, 4–23.

ROONEY, B. (1987) *Racism and Resistance to Change: A Study of the Black Social Workers Project in Liverpool SSD*, Liverpool: Sociology Department, Liverpool University.

ROONEY, B. and MCKAIN, J. (1990) *Voluntary Health Organisations and the Black Community in Liverpool*, Report of a survey by Health and Race Project, Liverpool: Sociology Department, Liverpool University.

ROYS, P. (1988) 'Racism and welfare: social services', in ASHOK BHAT, CARR-HILL, R. and SUSHEL OHRI (eds), *Britain's Black Population, A New Perspective*, Aldershot: Gower.

NALINI SADHOO (1990) 'Endless strife', *Social Work Today*, 21, 50, 15–17.

PARVITER SANGHERA (1990) 'A many headed beast', *The Health Service Journal*, 100, 5217, 1322.

ANURADHA SAYAL (1990) 'Black women and mental health', *The Psychologist*, January, 24–7.

SCHOFIELD, Z. (1988) 'Derby's bid to break down ethnic barrier', *The Health Service Journal*, 98, 5115, 963.

SCOTT, M. (1988) 'Racism in the fabric', *Social Work Today*, 20, 6, 42.

SEDLEY, A. (1989) *The Challenge of Anti Racism: Lessons from a Voluntary Organisation*, London: Family Service Units.

NEELAM SHARMA (1992) *Race and Disability: A Dialogue for Action*, London: GLAD.

SHAW, C. (1988) 'Latest estimates of ethnic minority populations', *Population Trends*, 51, 5–8.

SIMMEL, G. (1971) *On Individual and Social Forms*, Chicago: The University of Chicago Press.

SMITH, C. and STIFF, J. (1985) 'Problems of inner city general practice in North East London', *Journal of Royal College of General Practitioners*, 35, 71–6.

SMITH, P. (1988) 'Meeting the housing needs of elderly Asian people', *Social Work Today*, 19, 22, 9.

THE STANDING CONFERENCE OF ETHNIC MINORITY SENIOR CITIZENS (1991) *Breaking New Ground: Assessment of the Needs and Difficulties of Elderly House Bound and Disabled People among Ethnic Minorities*, London: SCEMSC.

STEVENS, K.A. and FLETCHER, R.F. (1989) 'Communicating with Asian patients', *British Medical Journal*, 6704, 905–6.

STOCKING, B. (1990) 'Health services for black and ethnic minorities', *King's Fund News*, 13, 3, 1.

STUBBS, P. (1985) 'The employment of black social workers: from "ethnic sensitivity" to anti racism?', *Critical Social Policy*, 4, 3, 6–27.

SUGDEN, M. (1988) 'Future agenda for issues of race', *Social Work Today*, 19, 36, 9.

TAMESIDE BLACK ELDERLY WORKING GROUP (1987) *The Black Elderly in Tameside*, Tameside: Tameside Metropolitan Borough Council.

TAMESIDE METROPOLITAN BOROUGH COUNCIL EQUAL OPPORTUNITIES UNIT (1989) *The Provision of Services to Black Elderly People in Tameside*, Tameside: Tameside Metropolitan Borough Council.

TARPEY, M. (1990) 'Ageing in ethnic minority groups, service provision to elderly people from black and minority ethnic groups', *Generations*, 14, 1–6.

TAYLOR, D. and MAYNARD, A. (1990) *Medicines, the NHS and Europe*, London: King's Fund Institute/Centre for Health Economics.

TONKIN, B. (1987) 'Black and blue', *Community Care*, 660, 18–20.

TORKINGTON, N.P.K. (1983) *The Racial Politics of Health – A Liverpool Profile*, Liverpool: Merseyside Area Profile Group, Sociology Department, University of Liverpool.

TOWNSEND, D. and ETHERINGTON, S. (1988) 'Progress: what progress?', *Social Services Insight*, 3, 2, 12–14.

TOWNSEND, P. and DAVIDSON, N. (1982) *Inequalities in Health*, Harmondsworth: Penguin.

TURNBULL, A.M. (1985) *Greenwich's Afro/Caribbean and South Asian Elderly People*, Greenwich: Greenwich Social Services Department.

TWIGG, J. (1989) 'Not taking the strain', *Community Care*, 773, 16–18.

TWIGG, J. (ed) (1992) *Carers: Research and Practice*, London: HMSO.

TWIGG, J. and ATKIN, K. (1993) *Carers Perceived: Policy and Practice in Informal Care*, Buckingham: Open University Press.

TWIGG, J., ATKIN, K. and PERRING, C. (1990) *Evaluating Support to Informal Carers (Part 1): Final Report*, DHSS 709 11.90, Social Policy Research Unit, York: University of York.

JANJIT UPPAL (1988) 'Helping Asian families in Smethwick', *Carelink*, 4, 3.

VIGILANCE, G. (1986) *Ethnic Minority Senior Citizens: A Question of Policy*, London: Standing Conference of Ethnic Minority Senior Citizens.

WAGNER, G. (1988) *Residential Care: A Positive Choice. Report of the Independent Review of Residential Care*, London: HMSO.

WALKER, C. (1987) 'How a survey led to providing more responsive help for Asian families', *Social Work Today*, 19, 7, 12–13.

WALLACE, L. (1991) *Black Carers – An Issues Paper*, Unpublished, Birmingham: Department of Social Studies, Selly Oak Colleges.

WARD, L. (1990) 'Blinded by the light', *Community Care*, 823, 18–19.

WATSON, E. (1984) 'Health of infants and use of health services by mothers of different ethnic groups in East London', *Community Medicine*, 6, 127–35.

WHITEHEAD, M. (1987) *The Health Divide: Inequalities in Health in the 1980s*, London: London Health Education Authority.

WHITFIELD, J.S. (1990) *Inspection into the Arrangements made for the Provision of Social Services to People from Minority Ethnic Groups by the SSDs in Bradford, Kirklees, Leeds and Sheffield*, London: Social Services Inspectorate (Yorkshire and Humberside Region).

WILKIN, D. and WILLIAMS, E.I. (1986) 'Patterns of care for the elderly in general practice', *Journal of the Royal College of General Practitioners*, 36, 567–70.

WILLIAMS, A. (1990) 'Contract friendly or contract deadly?' *NVCO Community Care Project – Newsletter* 17, 23–4.

WILLIAMS, F. (1989) *Issues of Race, Gender and Class: A Critical Introduction*, Oxford: Polity Press.

WILLIAMS, R. (1988) 'The black experience of social services', *Social Work Today*, 19, 19, 14–15.

WILSON, I. and MCGLOIN, P. (1989) 'Ethnic record keeping is not just ticking boxes', *Social Work Today*, 21, 5, 16–17.

WILSON, M. (1989) 'Equal service for a multi-racial community', *Social Work Today*, 20, 43, 15–17.

WILSON, M. (1990) 'Dr B's recipe for minority tastes', *Social Work Today*, 21, 40, 28–9.

WILSON, M. (1992) 'Forgotten people', *Social Work Today*, June, 17–20.

WRIGHT, C. (1983) 'Language and communication problems in an Asian Community', *Journal of Royal College of General Practitioners*, 33, 101–4.

WRIGHT, R. (1990) *Social Services and Members of Black and Minority Ethnic Communities: A Report of a Workshop*, London: Social Services Inspectorate.

YEBOAH, F. and PALMER, S. (eds) (1987) *The LARRIE Catalogue – A Listing of Local Authority Papers on Racial Equality*, London: Local Authorities Race Relations Information Exchange.

YEE, L. (1991) 'Responding to black carers' needs', *Carer*, 16, 7–10.

YOUNG, C. (1990) 'Black and ethnic minority users and carers in rural areas', *ARVAC Bulletin*, Winter 43, 4–5.

ZAMORA, M. (1988) 'Black carers in Haringey', *Carelink*, 4, 2.

# Index

Afro-Caribbean community 3, 7
  age structure of 8
  disabilities of 10
  experience of GPs of 26
  families in 14–15
  knowledge of services of 19, 21–8
  use of English by 16
  use of social services by 21
age
  and disability 10
  of minority groups 8, 68
Age Concern, service to ethnic
  minorities 54
Age Concern Institute of
  Gerontology 29
Ahmad, B. 30, 50
Ahmad, W.I.U. 31, 36, 39, 47
anti-racist methodology 67–72
Asian community 3, 7
  age structure of 8
  disabilities of 10, 69
  employment of 43, 45
  experience of GPs of 26
  family networks in 13–14
  GPs' perceptions of 38–9
  help from voluntary agencies 53–4
  knowledge of services of 19, 21–8
  language of 16, 47
  male carers among 15
  and social services 21, 33
  use of respite care 23–4
Asian day centres 23
Asian Mother and Baby Campaign 69
Athwal, S. 75
Atkin, K. 13, 15, 20, 21, 23, 26, 74

Badger, F. 27, 39
Baldwin, S. 15
Ballard, R. 72
Bangladeshi community 8
Barker, J. 15–16, 73
Batley 43
Baxter, C. 12, 13, 16, 19, 41–42, 75

Begum, N. 11, 12
Berry, S. 14, 73
Best, C. 50
Bhaduri, R. 33, 34, 76
Bhalla, A. 13, 14, 18, 21, 26, 73
Bhat, A. 38
Bhopal, R.S. 10
Bingley, W. 38
Birmingham
  black population in 9
  CCSAP 13
  use of community services by black
    people in 20
black minorities 3, 63–4
  composition of 7–9
  disability among 9–11, 64
  experience of community nursing
    services 27
  experience of GPs 26
  knowledge and use of statutory
    services 19–28
  stereotyping of 30–1, 68–70
  *see also* Afro-Caribbean community;
    Asian community
black pathology 30–1, 38, 68
black people 67–8
  and community care 71–2
  employment of 41–5
black voluntary organisations 23, 58,
  61, 66
  expectations of 60
  financial resources of 58–9
  relationship with statutory
    services 59–60
Blakemore, K. 13, 14, 18, 26, 73
Bould, M. 16, 17, 24
Bradford Social Services
  Department 58
Brent, London Borough of 9
British Association of Social Work 32
British Medical Association 68
Brown, C. 18
Bulsara, S. 75

Burke, A. 38
Butt, J. 76

Camden, London Borough of 24, 75
Cameron, E. 14, 15, 16, 39
Cancerlink 13
carer support groups 25
Carers Unit 12–13
change
   commitment to 50
   in voluntary agencies  56, 57
Chauhan, B. 14
chiropody 28
Chowdhury, A. 70
Cocking, I. 75
Cole, J. 75
Commission for Racial Equality 33,
   34, 41, 45, 46, 76
communication difficulties 16, 30, 31
   in respite care 24
community care, and race 1–2, 70–2
Community Care Special Action
   Project 13
community nursing services 26–7
   racism in 39–40
community service provision 19, 70–2
   black people's experiences of 66
   knowledge of 19–28
see also health services; social services
Confederation of Indian
   Organisations, 11
Connelly, N. 49, 50, 57
Conroy, S. 37
consultation rates 26
continence services 27–8
Coombe, V. 14
Crossroads Care Attendant
   schemes 24–25
cultural diversity 30–2, 67–9
cultural factors, in GP consultation
   rates 26
culture, of black people 31, 67–9
   health visitors' perception of 39
   and short term care 24
   and white culture 67
Cypher, J. 76

Daniel, S. 59
day care provision
   knowledge of 22–3
   reservations about 23
Dearnley, J. 76
dementia 27

Department of Health 34, 35
   Caring for People 1
Derbyshire Family Practitioner
   Committee 35
Dewsbury 43
Dimsdale, Len 42
disability, among black people 9–11,
   64
disadvantage
   of black people 26
   of older people 68
discrimination 34, 41
   in voluntary sector 54
distribution of black populations 8–9
district nurses, attitude to black
   people 39
doctors see GPs
Donaldson, L.J. 10, 18, 25
Donovan, J. 26
Dourado, P. 12
Dungate, M. 55, 56, 77
Durrant, J. 30, 31, 42, 50
Dutt, R. 50

Ebrahim, S. 10
emotional cost, of care 15–17
employment of black people 41–3
   and caring 17
English, use of in black
   communities 16, 23
equal opportunity policies 33–4, 42–3,
   50
   in health services 35–6, 44–5
   in voluntary sector 56, 66
Eribo, L. 15, 75
Etherington, S. 46, 76
ethnic diversity 67–9
ethnic minorities see black minorities
ethnic minority development
   workers 51–2
ethnic monitoring 45–6, 66
ethnicity 3–4, 7–9, 63–4
   and isolation of caring 15–16
Evers, H. 31, 76
extended family 13, 14, 31

family life, disruption of through
   caring 16–17
family networks 13–15, 31
   caring within 15
family structure, changes in 14
Farleigh, A. 59
Farrah, M. 11, 14, 15, 18

Fenton, S. 13, 14, 25, 74
Field, S. 53, 54, 57, 60
financial costs, of caring 17
financial resources, for black voluntary
  organisations 58–9
Foleshill Mental Handicap Survey 28
food 22, 23
Foster, M.C. 31, 39, 40, 76

gender, of elderly in black
  communities 8
General Household Survey 11–18,
  64–5
general practice, racism in 38–9
general practitioners
  Asian 39
  and language barrier 47
  treatment of ethnic minorities 26
  use of by black people 25–6
Gillam, S.J. 26
Glendenning, F. 36, 58, 60
Goel, K.M. 68
Green, H. 10, 11
Griffiths, R. 1
Grimsley, M. 38
Gulliford, F. 16, 17
Gunaratnum, Y. 75

Halahmy, R. 50
Hameed, A. 38
Haringey Health Authority 51
Haskey, J. 7, 8
health, of black people 9–11, 68–9
health authorities
  equal opportunity policies in 35–6,
    44–5
  policy and practice of 34–5, 51–2
health education 31
health services 25–8
  employment of black workers
    in 44–5
  ethnic monitoring in 46
  and ethnicity 51–2
  knowledge of, among black
    people 19
  language barrier and 47–8
  provision to black people 34–5, 36,
    66
  racism in 36–7
  use of by black people 20
health visitors 31
  and racism 39–40
Hicks, C. 12

Holland, B. 10, 19
home help service 21, 32
housing, for black people 17–18
Hughes, R. 33, 34, 76

incomes, of black people 17, 68
individual racism 4, 29–30
  in community nursing 39–40
  in general practice 38
informal care, in black
  communities 11–8, 64–5
informal carers 11–12, 13, 65
  visibility of 12–13
institutional racism 4, 11, 29, 30
  in health services 36–7, 51–2
  in social services 49–51
interpreters 47
interpreting services 47–8
isolation, of caring 15–16

Jackson, H. 53, 54, 57, 60, 74
Johnson, M. 73
Jowell, T. 75

Kalsi, N. 51
Kapur, R.L. 17
King, V.I.H. 68
King's Fund 12–13, 35, 51
Kiple, K.F. 68
knowledge, lack of 16
knowledge of services 19–28

Lalljie, R. 58
language 31,47
learning difficulties 10, 24, 28
Lee, M. 23, 24, 75
Leicester, Asian carers in 12, 18
Liverpool
  Health and Race Project survey
    in 56
  home help service in 32
  Muslim meals service in 22
living conditions, and health 11
Lewando-Hundt, G. 10, 19
luncheon clubs 22
Lunn, T. 13

McAvoy, B.R. 9, 16
McCalman, J.A. 11–12, 15, 16, 21, 27,
  28, 75
McDonald, P. 19
McFarland, E. 21, 22, 74

McGloin, P. 46
McNaught, A. 36, 44, 51, 52
mainstream voluntary sector 54–7
    and future policy 57, 66
Mallinson, I. 50
Martin, J. 10
May, A. 60
Maynard, A. 26
meals on wheels 21–2
medication, misuse of 47
mental health 10, 27, 64
    racism and 37–8
migration 30
    and family division 14
Milner, I.W. 76
Mohammed, S. 37
Moledina, S. 39, 74

Naik, D. 33
National Association of Health
    Authorities 36, 37, 51
National Council of Voluntary
    Organisations (NCVO) 55
needs, of black people 70, 71
Newton, T. 34
NHS see health services
NHS and Community Care Act,
    1990 1
non-verbal communication 16
Norman, A. 47, 54
nursing see community nursing
    services

occupational therapy 21
occupations, and health 11
Odell, A. 18, 25
Oldman, C. 18
OPCS 10, 64
Owusu-Bempah, J. 50

Pai, S. 17
Pakistani community 8
Parker, G. 13, 15
Patel, M. 12
Patel, N. 60
Pearson, M. 10, 19, 33, 36, 44, 58, 60
Phaure, S. 77
Phipps, R. 19
physical cost, of caring 15
physiotherapy 28
Policy Studies Institute 11, 16
Prime, R. 76

psychiatric institutions, black people
    in 31, 38
psychiatric nurses 27
psychological jeopardy 14
publicity, of voluntary services 56

race 3
    and community care 1–2, 70–2
    and community service
        provision 65–6
    and disability 10–11
    and health service provision 35
    language of 2
race advisers, in health authorities 51
Race Relations Act, 1976 42
race research 67–70
racism 4, 67
    in community nursing 39–40
    in mental health 37–8
    and service provision 29–30, 31,
        36–37, 66
    in voluntary sector 54, 57
    see also individual racism;
        institutional racism
relationships, stress in, through
    caring 16–17
research, among black
    communities 67–70, 71
respite care 23–4
Roach, D. 42
Robinson, J. 23, 24
Rocheron, Y. 68–9
Rooney, B. 32, 77
Roys, P. 44

Scott, M. 32
Sedley, A. 56
sitting services, reservations of black
    carers about 24–5
Smith, P. 38
social control 31–2
social security benefits 17
social service departments 41
    employment of black workers in
        43–4
    equal opportunity policies of 33–4,
        66
    and ethnic minority users 32–3,
        49–51
    ethnic monitoring in 46
    race and 49, 50, 65–6

social services 57
  black people's experiences of 30,
    31–2
  policy and practice of 32–3
Social Services Inspectorate 33, 43
social work 20–1
social workers, attitude to black
  clients 30–1, 34
Southwark, London Borough of,
  survey of carers in 11–12, 15, 18
special need 70, 71
special therapy 28
Standing Conference of Ethnic
  Minority Senior Citizens 19, 59
stereotypes 30–1, 38, 39, 56
Stiff, J. 38
Stocking, B. 51
Stubbs, P. 42

Tameside, survey in (1987) 10, 74
Taylor, D. 26
tokenism 42
Tonkin, B. 38

Townsend, D. 46, 76
translation of leaflets 47, 56

voluntary agencies, knowledge and
  use of 53–4, 66–7
  see also black voluntary
    organisations

Walker, C. 15, 16, 75
Wallace, L. 75
West Lambeth Health Authority 52
White Paper on Commonwealth
  Immigration (1965) 68
Wilkin, D. 26
Williams, E.I. 26
Williams, R. 31
Wilson, M. 46
women, as carers 15, 16
Wright, C. 38, 47, 76

Yee, L. 12

Zamora, M. 16

Printed in the United Kingdom for HMSO
Dd296523 7/93 C11 G531 10170